Exploring the Benefits of Numerical Simulation and Modelling

Edited by Mykhaylo I. Andriychuk

Published in London, United Kingdom

Exploring the Benefits of Numerical Simulation and Modelling
http://dx.doi.org/10.5772/intechopen.1002095
Edited by Mykhaylo I. Andriychuk

Contributors
Abd Raouf Chouikha, Adrian C. Eide, Mykhaylo Andriychuk, Pavel Loskot, Qijing Yang, Sergey Martyushov, Victor Tkachuk

First published in London, United Kingdom, 2025 by IntechOpen
IntechOpen is the global imprint of INTECHOPEN LIMITED, registered in England and Wales, registration number: 11086078, 167-169 Great Portland Street, London, W1W 5PF, United Kingdom

For EU product safety concerns: IN TECH d.o.o., Prolaz Marije Krucifikse Kozulić 3, 51000 Rijeka, Croatia, info@intechopen.com or visit our website at intechopen.com.

British Library Cataloguing-in-Publication Data
A catalogue record for this book is available from the British Library

Exploring the Benefits of Numerical Simulation and Modelling
Edited by Mykhaylo I. Andriychuk
p. cm.
Print ISBN 978-0-85466-830-4
Online ISBN 978-0-85466-829-8
eBook (PDF) ISBN 978-0-85466-831-1

If disposing of this product, please recycle the paper responsibly.

Meet the editor

Prof. Andriychuk received an MSc in Computational Mathematics from Lviv National University, a Ph. D. in Application of Computational Techniques from Kyiv National University, and a DSc in Mathematical Modelling from Lviv Polytechnic National University (LPNU) in Ukraine in 1976, 1987, and 2015, respectively. He has been with the Pidstryhach Institute for Applied Problems of Mechanics and Mathematics (IAPMM), Lviv, Ukraine, for 48 years. Currently, he is the Head of the Department at IAPMM and a professor at LPNU. His professional performance includes about 200 papers in scientific journals and international conference proceedings concerning diffraction and antenna synthesis theory, optimization methods, and nonlinear integral equations. He is also the author of four books on antenna synthesis theory. He has been an Institute of Electrical and Electronics Engineers (IEEE) Member since 1995 and IEEE Senior Member since 2003.

Contents

Preface

Numerical simulation and modelling are powerful tools that allow for exploring a series of natural and industry phenomena, gaining a portion of their important properties, which can be applied to improve our knowledge about environmental processes. This field of investigation exploits inevitable recipes to understand the universe, from the behaviour of atomic particles to the dynamics of giant space objects.

The book collects the recent research related to numerical simulation and modelling in the areas of theoretical physics, fluid mechanics, geo-techniques, pure and computational mathematics, random processes, and satellite communications. As is customary, the problems are considered, starting with developing a mathematical model of the process/phenomenon under consideration and ending with constructing algorithms and software tools to get the numerical results that contribute to a better understanding of its nature and obtaining new knowledge about it.

In Chapter 1, A. C. Eide introduces a physical principle of vacuum diagram loop divergence treatment using the analytic continuation in conjunction with the proposed inherent physical property of virtual quantization. It has been established that such an approach supplemented by a set of properties inherent in the object of study allows associating a finite negative zero-point energy. It turns out that the proposed physical principle is a useful practical and mathematically equivalent way to interpret the Casimir effect. Some examples of the application of the examined physical principle are outlined; mainly, it shows its application to the conformally flat de-Sitter case. A pattern of the quantitative implications of this model is demonstrated in the frame of clarity and completeness. Important discussions on the most critical sources of error and ill-posseness are mentioned, and practical recipes to avoid the appearing shortcomings are made.

Chapter 2, authored by S. Martyushov, is devoted to the numerical investigation of the flows of reactive gas mixes in obstacle channels to define regimes of deflagration initiation. The numerical simulation of these phenomena is very important because it prevents accidents that may occur during the operation of the hydrogen machines. For numerical simulation of reactive gas mix flows, the system of ideal gas equations for 2D flows is given in an integral form for finite volume cell; the source term presents the velocities of changing gas mix components via chemical reaction in the right-hand part of this system. The non-linear TVD difference scheme is applied to solve these equations numerically. The chemical kinetic model supplements the consideration relatively to the correctness of the approach proposed. The presented simulation data correspond well with the physics of turbulent flows.

Q. Yang, in Chapter 3, considers the application of numerical modelling to solve complex geotechnical problems related to the assessment of building constructions. The approach foresees problems considering a series of natural conditions, such as geotechnical and hydro-geological design parameters, which are of definitive importance when investigating objects in the natural environment. The research starts with developing a conceptual ground model based on a set of fundamental parameters such as the soil, rock, and water behaviours under various boundary and loading conditions. Two types of buildings, such as the piled bridge abutment and metro shaft excavation, are studied. The first case study foresees the development of procedures for numerical modelling of geotechnical problems, new bridge concept and detail design development, geotechnical investigations and ground model, assessment of a single pile capacity, pile group analysis using Piglet Software, Plaxis 3D analysis and results evaluation, and engineering realization based on the obtained modelling data. The second case study starts with site investigations, model development, and the specification of model parameters. The construction staging and 2D and 3D results of independent numerical modelling are the forthcoming steps. Modelling observations and discussions, instrumentation and monitoring of the object under investigation, and construction control and site validation finish this case. The modelling results are presented comprehensively.

In Chapter 4, A. R. Chouikha proposes the one-parameter trigonometric and hyperbolic inequalities chain approach to simplify a series of basic algebraic relations. The research starts with an introduction to the classical trigonometry inequalities, which are applied widely in engineering design. A series of theorems allow for establishing important relations between the sets of trigonometric functions. All theorems are proven to enable the use of reduced relations in engineering practice. The theorems are extended in the case of hyperbolic functions. The perspective of the approach is an extension of the results in the case of a real number of terms in the considered relations.

The random processes defined by stochastic differential and difference equations are investigated by P. Loskot in Chapter 5. The study started by describing the various linear and non-linear processes, which are described in terms of the statistical differential equations. An explanation of how the continuous and discrete models are interconnected is given. The steps of passing from the nonlinear model to the linear one are also discussed. The recipe to get the analytical representation of the solution to the stochastic differential equation in the form of the Cramer integral representation is shown. The explanation of how the non-linear model can be obtained from the linear one introducing a non-linear measurement equation with the added measurement noise is given. The general linear model of a non-stationary random process was presented to derive a Kalman filter for estimating the extended vector of parameters. The partial random cases of processes, such as the binominal counting process, Poisson process, Wiener process, and multivariable Gaussian process, following from this generalization, are discussed. A short description of the numerical methods for solving the derived stochastic differential equations is given, and examples of generating the random processes are shown.

M. Andriychuk and V. Tkachuk, in Chapter 6, propose a variational statement of the optimization problem for a 3D linear array, which forms radiation in a far zone. The subsequent application of the optimization procedure, which consists of applying a gradient method of successive approximation to its solving, is examined. The linear array is built of the source of excitation, the inclined semitransparent plane mirrors, and the final metallic mirror are studied. The quasi-optical condition applies to the geometry of the array. The distance between the array's adjacent elements satisfies the Fresnel zone's conditions, and its radiation pattern (RP) is determined in a far zone. The authors assume that the variables are separated in the planes of mirrors and the RP in the far zone. The close formulas are derived for the field in the array mirrors and the created RP. The numerical computations demonstrate a rapid convergence of the iterative method used and the possibility of the array forming the radiation characteristics that satisfy the different engineering demands.

I am pleased to thank all book authors for their enthusiasm, effort, and improvement of the chapters throughout the review process. In addition, I express my sincere thanks to Ms. Karmen Daleta for her professional support during the book preparation.

Mykhaylo Andriychuk
Pidstryhach Institute for Applied Problems of Mechanics and Mathematics, NASU,
Lviv Polytechnic National University,
Lviv, Ukraine

Chapter 1

A Case for the Application of Analytic Continuation in Physics

Adrian C. Eide

Abstract

This chapter will motivate the introduction of one proposed physical principle of vacuum diagram loop divergence treatment by analytic continuation in conjunction with the proposed inherent physical property of virtual quantization. And show that when such a proposed principle and proposed property are adopted that it becomes possible to associate a finite negative zero-point energy. This proposed physical principle is shown to be a useful or practical and mathematically equivalent way of interpreting the Casimir effect. Some examples of the application of this proposed physical principle are outlined, in particular its application to the conformally flat de-Sitter case. An outline of the quantitative implications of this model is tabled for the sake of clarity and completeness. Important discussions on the most critical sources of error and falsification are mentioned, and concrete predictions made.

Keywords: analytic continuation, vacuum diagram loop divergences, virtual quantization, applications, the Casimir effect

1. Introduction

The quest for the unifying principles of physics started with the work of many brilliant minds more than 50 years ago as of the time of writing of this chapter. In 1973, it was shown [1] by Bekenstein that for the case of black holes, where the principles of physics meet, that it is natural and necessary to consider that its entropy be proportional to the surface area of the black hole and not its volume. Less than a year later, in 1974, Hawking [2] found a way to show that black holes are not perfectly black and must radiate thermally due to quantum effects. The consequence of their work, (and others) was that due to the fact that the internal energy could only originate from the black hole mass and not from other known sources of energy that black holes must evaporate with time and eventually disappear completely, and thus that all the quantum information that falls in would eventually be lost to our universe. More precisely, as recently reviewed by Calmet and Hsu [3] that black holes cause pure states to evolve into mixed states. This paradox came to be known as the information paradox. Approximately at the same time, as an attempt at finding these unifying principles, it was shown by Davies [4] and independently by Unruh [5] that any uniformly accelerated observer in a vacuum field will experience a thermal bath.

The equivalence principle provides the bridge between this Unruh-Davies effect and the Hawking radiation at a black hole's surface.

Ever since the seventies and eighties, there have been many other interesting proposals and developments as for the fundamental, unifying principles, and consequent theories of physics. One of the most promising attempts at this was the development of string theory, built on the work by Veneziano [6], and many others. The use of analytic continuation as a way to treat divergences is often used in string theory, for example, as demonstrated by D'Hoker and Phong [7]. As far as the author of this chapter understands, the issue of the arising vacuum diagram loop divergences in physical calculations is a remaining problem today. This motivates an attempt at introducing a unifying physical principle of how to treat these vacuum diagram loop divergences in general.

In this context, a special topic of interest is the case of virtual particles. As reviewed by Lamoreaux [8], the Casimir effect or Casimir force is known to be an attractive force between two uncharged material bodies (usually, thin parallel plates) due to the difference of the zero-point energies associated with said virtual particles on either side of said plates. This energy gradient generates a small and attractive force between the plates. This interpretation of the origins of the Casimir force originates from the treatment of the arising divergence by zeta regularization and consequent renormalization, a technique for subtracting away the divergence on either side of the plates, in order to be able to associate a finite, physically measured value by Mohideen and Anushree [9] and many others.

With these in mind, this chapter will begin by discussing the treatment of virtual divergences with regards to this effect. And how a different, mathematically equivalent interpretation may be more useful or practical as it comes to the general treatment of these vacuum diagram loop divergences by a proposed, unifying physical principle. This is important as a tool in order to develop an intuition of how this interpretation may be more generally applied. This discussion will later be expanded upon in order to include this plausible general interpretation, and how it applies to an example. The chapter will, then, be expanded further by a different example of the application of this proposed general principle, based on prior work [10] by the author of this chapter. The known immediate implications will be tabled for the sake of clarity and completeness and followed by a section (see Section 3) that will try to address and discuss some of the main issues of the proposed model, as well as offer possible methods of falsification. Finally, concrete predictions based on this proposed general principle of the treatment of vacuum diagram loop divergences will be made. In addition to some concrete predictions based on its implications as shown.

2. A brief outline of the thought process

In the underlying QFTs (see Abbreviations), the processes of regularization refer to the set of techniques known to obtain a finite result of divergent series or loop integrals. For an extensive overview of the various regularization methods see [11] by Kachelriess. What all these methods have in common is that they all try to get rid of arising divergences in various ways. This is part of the motivation of trying to find a unifying principle of how to treat arising vacuum diagram loop divergences in general. One attempt, it is possible to try is inspired by the method of zeta regularization. That is treating the arising vacuum diagram loop divergences by going beyond them instead of getting rid of them; in this way the introduction of regulators or cutoff parameters becomes redundant, and the arising divergences become treatable by analytic continuation. Next follows a discussion of this with regards to the Casimir effect.

2.1 Divergence treatment and the Casimir effect

The vacuum energy density $\rho(d)$ associated with virtual fluctuations per polarization mode in the 1 + 1 dimensional Casimir case has been shown by Kachelriess [12] and many others to lead to an equation of the form.

$$\rho(d) = \frac{\pi}{2d^2}\sum_{n=1}^{\infty} n \tag{1}$$

where d is the distance between the plates. In this case, the necessary virtual quantization

$$\omega_n = \frac{n\pi}{d} \tag{2}$$

follows from the boundary conditions of the wavefunction between the plates. The divergence of (Eq. (1)) is then treated by zeta regularization and renormalization, see [12] for details. After this divergence treatment, the final result is of the form.

$$\rho_{\zeta reg}(d) = -\frac{\pi}{24d^2} \tag{3}$$

And thus it is possible to obtain an energy distance gradient, and therefore an attractive Casimir force between the plates. This zero-point energy gradient is, thereby, interpreted to be the origins of the Casimir force.

Another useful or practical way to interpret the origins of the Casimir force in order to build a tentative intuition of the general divergence treatment in QFTs is by the application of the principle of vacuum diagram loop divergence treatment by analytic continuation and using the well-known result.

$$\sum_{n=1}^{\infty} n = \zeta(-1) = -\frac{1}{12} \tag{4}$$

The Riemann zeta function $\zeta(s)$ evaluated by analytic continuation at $s = -1$. It is noted that this is the identical sum as it appears in (Eq. (1)). Thus, by interpreting the treatment of the virtual divergence by analytic continuation (Eq. (4)), it becomes possible to avoid the introduction of a cutoff function and go beyond the divergence instead of trying to get rid of it as follows

$$\rho_{\zeta}(d) = \frac{\pi}{2d^2}\sum_{n=1}^{\infty} n = \frac{\pi}{2d^2}\left(-\frac{1}{12}\right) = -\frac{\pi}{24d^2} = \rho_{\zeta reg}(d) \tag{5}$$

which is mathematically equivalent to the regularization treatment and interpretation, which it must be for consistency.

Therefore, according to this interpretation, the Casimir force does not originate from the zero-point energy gradient across the plates but rather originates from an inherent proposed physical principle applied to the virtual fluctuations in the space itself, which then exists independently of the presence of the finite Casimir cavity. The inherent proposed physical principle is the principle of the treatment of the vacuum diagram loop divergences by analytic continuation. In other words, the effect is inherently present and can only be changed in magnitude by finite cavity manipulations.

2.2 General discussions on the proposed inherent physical principle of vacuum diagram loop divergence treatment by analytic continuation

When describing the motion of a free scalar field $\phi(x_i)$ in free field theory, a function of interest is often the Green's function. The reason for this is because the Green's function can be used as a mathematical tool to solve difficult EOMs (see Nomenclature). In said free field theory, a typical general calculation usually ends up with trying to derive the n-point Green's function $G^{(n)}(x_1, \ldots, x_n)$ described by an infinite sum over all loop orders, the first loop order contribution is (see **Figure 1**).

Where the vacuum diagram loop propagation without external lines is described by the Euclidean Feynman loop propagator after Wick rotation.

$$i\Delta_F(0) = \frac{1}{(2\pi)^4} \int_{-\infty}^{\infty} \frac{d^4 k_E}{k_E^2 + m^2} \tag{6}$$

where it was reiterated in [10] that in order to obtain the desired Weyl invariance it is necessary that $m = 0$. Thus, the divergent Feynman loop integral simplifies to

$$i\Delta_F(0) = \frac{1}{(2\pi)^4} \int_0^{\infty} \frac{dk_E 2\pi^2 k_E^3}{k_E^2} = \frac{1}{8\pi^2} \int_0^{\infty} dk_E k_E \tag{7}$$

which is the divergent vacuum diagram loop integral of interest. It is noted that due to the fact that the discussion is concerning periodic loop diagrams, and thus that there may be a standard periodicity of the field $\phi(x_i)$

$$\phi(x_i + L) = \phi(x) \rightarrow e^{ik_E(x_i+L)} = e^{ik_E x_i} \tag{8}$$

which implies

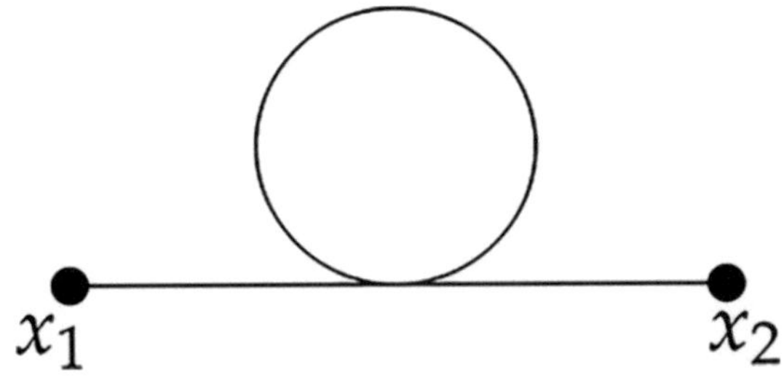

Figure 1.
The loop diagram of interest to first order with an external line.

$$e^{ik_E L} = 1 = e^{i2\pi n} \rightarrow k_E = \frac{2\pi n}{L}, n \in \mathbb{N} \tag{9}$$

For the n-th mode. Thus, it can be argued that virtual particles which are by definition associated with closed-loop diagrams, and therefore must have periodic boundary conditions with some periodic lengthscale L independent of the spacetime background they are embedded in necessarily have to have a quantized wavenumber as shown.

Therefore, it is plausible that the origins of the quantization are inherent to the virtual particle system by definition, and thus may exist independently of the presence of a finite Casimir cavity. Using this proposed physical inherent property and the proposed general principle of vacuum diagram loop divergence treatment by analytical continuation, it becomes possible to conveniently avoid the introduction of a regulator and instead go beyond the divergence to obtain a result for the vacuum diagram loop integral of interest (Eq. (7))

$$i\Delta_F(0) = \frac{1}{8\pi^2}\int_0^\infty dk_E k_E = \frac{1}{4\pi L}\sum_{n=0}^{\infty} n = \frac{1}{4\pi L}\left(-\frac{1}{12}\right) = -\frac{1}{48\pi L} \tag{10}$$

For some periodic lengthscale L. Thus, it becomes possible to associate a finite and negative zero-point energy contribution in flat Euclidean geometry. It was shown [10] that the application of the proposed physical inherent property of virtual quantization (which may or may not be true for all possible spacetimes) together with the proposed principle of vacuum diagram loop divergence treatment by analytic continuation can with internal consistency be extended to the case of a conformally flat dS spacetime as observed by any inertial observer. This application and subsequent immediate implications of this will be discussed next.

2.3 The application of the general principle of vacuum diagram loop divergence treatment by analytic continuation to the conformally flat dS case

The proposed general principle of vacuum diagram loop divergence treatment by analytic continuation in conjunction with the proposed plausible property of inherent virtual quantization was shown in detail [10] with internal consistency to lead to a zero-point energy E_0 within an implicit unit space $L = 1$ m, see Section 3.1 for an error discussion on this to be.

$$E_0 = -\frac{\pi}{6} < 0 \tag{11}$$

Converting to SI units and making the critical observation of the presence of a $\hbar c$ factor, which may account for the scaling required in the relevant conformally flat dS case, and finally squaring for dimensional analysis.

$[\Lambda_{dS}] = \mathrm{m}^{-2}$ yields the critical scaling

$$\boxed{\Lambda_{dS} \propto \hbar^2 c^2} \tag{12}$$

Where the exact value of the geometrical proportionality constant remains to be determined with accuracy but is expected to be of order $O(-1)$. The critical observation that the proposed principle of vacuum diagram loop divergence treatment by analytic continuation in the conformally flat dS case and indeed for the Minkowski case, as well as shown in the previous Section 2.2 leads to the desired 52 zeros in SI units within an order of magnitude compared to the Planck data [13] was the original motivation for the proposition of this physical principle. For a more detailed derivation of this see [10].

2.4 Immediate implications of the principle of vacuum diagram loop divergence treatment by analytic continuation applied to the conformally flat dS case

It is plausible to argue that the simplest possible hypothesis is that the conformally flat dS cosmology attempted to be described here is identical to an internal Schwarzschild geometry (see Appendix A and [10] for quick derivations with regards to this). All the immediate implications are tabled (see **Table 1**) for the sake of clarity and completeness. A final less immediate interpretation of another implication is briefly outlined in [16], interpreting the Hubble scale as identical to a quantum uncertainty in position, and therefore may provide a mechanism for why there is something rather than nothing. It is quite possible there are even more unknown implications here, and more work is needed to outline them if they exist.

Quantitative relation in SI units	Name or context	Physical interpretation
$\Lambda_{dS} \propto \hbar^2 c^2$	*Lagrange multiplier.*	*Zero-point energy squared in dS spacetime.*
$\rho_{dS} \propto \frac{\hbar^2 c^6}{G}$	*Ideal fluid model.*	*Default vacuum energy density in dS spacetime.*
$R \propto \frac{1}{\hbar c}$	*Spatial observable cosmological scale today.*	*Current Hubble scale, that is. the radius to the current cosmological event horizon.*
$M \propto \frac{c}{\hbar G}$	*Massive observable cosmological scale today.*	*Baryonic matter (or effective matter, that is including the dark matter) of the observable cosmological scale today.*
$a_{dS} \propto \hbar c^3$	*Dark energy.*	*Repulsive acceleration due to virtual vacuum fluctuations in dS spacetime.*
$v^4 \propto \hbar G c^3 M$	*Tully-Fisher relation* [14]	*Galaxy mechanics.*
$w = -1 < -\frac{1}{3}$	*Black hole singularity theorems.*	*The presence of an EOS* $w = -1 < -\frac{1}{3}$ *counteracts the gravitational collapse* [15], *and thus resolves the black hole physical singularity.*
$M^2 \propto \left(\frac{c}{\hbar G}\right)^2$	*Plausible baryon mass symmetry breaking mechanism.*	$M = 0$ *is not a global minima of the energy function (Eq. (13)), but it rather has two global minima. Presumably corresponding to the matter vs. antimatter solutions.*
$dS = -\frac{p_{dS} dV}{T} > 0$	*Information paradox.*	*The cosmological entropy is encoded at its surface, the presence of another energy source suggests that the internal energy need not originate from the black hole mass M, and thus does not need to evaporate with time, but expands with time at all times.*

Table 1.
Table of relations, context, and physical interpretations of said proposed model.

3. Error discussion and methods of falsification

This section will discuss plausible errors of this analysis and end with mentioning possible methods of falsification. The error discussion will focus on two main critical points: the arbitrary chosen $L = 1$ m value and the issue of covariance.

3.1 L = 1 m WLOG

One objection made is the issue of the arbitrary chosen $L = 1$ m value, and how this can have anything to do with the general cosmological scale. It is of course true that for the proposed model and principle to be physical, that its empirically correlated output must be invariant under our arbitrary chosen size of unit of measurement. As far as the author of this chapter understands as of its time of writing, it is thought that the role of the periodic L lengthscale, in addition to being a measure of the cavity dimension if such a cavity is present at all as outlined in Section 2.1 is that it *defines the unit of measurement* used to derive the quantitative output (see Section 2.4). In other words, setting $L = 1$ m and only in this way, allows for the usage of the SI units measured values of the factor $\hbar c$. Setting L to an arbitrary value say α, such that $L = \alpha$ scales the unit of measurement by a factor α such that the then numerically measured value of $\hbar c$ changes by the same factor as compared with the SI unit $L = 1$ m value. Thus, the empirically correlated outputs become independent of the arbitrary scaling factor $L = \alpha$. Therefore, it seems possible to argue that the seemingly arbitrary choice of the value of $L = 1$ m is a choice WLOG as for the empirically correlated output.

However, as for the time of writing of this chapter, this concept or argument is not very well understood and quite possibly may turn out to be an erroneous argument. It is critical for the self-consistency of the proposed model (2.3) for it to be independent of the magnitude choice of the periodic lengthscale L. The desired output of the proposed conformally flat model (see Section 2.4) within an order of magnitude as compared with the Planck data [13] in addition to the Tully-Fisher relation [14] and other desired simultaneous implications as tabled makes it; as far as the author estimates more likely than not that the proposed conformally flat dS model is not a result of numerical conspiracy.

3.2 Covariance

Another source of error of this model is the matter of covariance. It was, however, shown in [10] that the result (Eq. (12)) for the conformally flat dS case only applies to all inertial reference frames. It is as of today unclear whether or not this relation and its immediate implications thereafter also hold true for all non-inertial reference frames. The inherent proposed physical property of virtual quantization by exploiting the loop periodicity by definition, as well as the proposed physical principle of said vacuum diagram loop divergence treatment by analytic continuation is proposed to be true in general, that is generally covariant. As far as the author of this chapter understands, it is not strictly necessary for the proposed model and principles to be generally covariant, that also holds true for all non-inertial reference frames since all the relevant data [13] were taken with the solar system as a (very good approximation) inertial frame of reference.

3.3 Possible methods of falsification

The following section will give a list of possible methods of falsification of this proposed physical principle. For instance, rigorously showing one of the following would be a valid falsification as far as the author of this chapter understands:

- Rigorously show that the default magnitude choice of the L periodic lengthscale does not maintain generality.
- Rigorously show that the proposed physical principle of vacuum diagram loop divergence treatment by analytic continuation will in a vacuum diagram case yield a pole. For example by getting a harmonic series ($s = 1$) in the analysis, which does not allow for analytic continuation.
- Rigorously show that the proposed inherent virtual quantization is not mathematically or physically consistent.
- Rigorously show that an as of today unknown implication or implications of said proposed principle gives empirical predictions that turn out to be incompatible with present or future data with statistical significance.
- Rigorously show that any one of the known implications is incompatible with present or future data with statistical significance. Given that the exact value of the geometrical proportionality constant is as of today yet to be determined, more than one order of magnitude deviation between these implications and any data with statistical significance will be considered critical.

As outlined in Section 3.2, it is not thought that the general showing of a lack of covariance of the proposed model would be a valid method of falsification since the conformally flat dS case (Eq. (12)) was only claimed [10] to hold for all inertial reference frames, and it remains unclear whether or not it is generally covariant.

3.4 Concrete predictions

The proposed model yields the following concrete predictions:

- Every vacuum diagram virtual loop divergence will *without exception* be treatable by analytic continuation, and the result will be identical to the physical result and hold true at least for all inertial reference frames.
- The quantization of virtual particle loops is an inherent physical property, and thus must exists independently of the presence of a Casimir cavity.

In addition to this, there are the following concrete predictions from its immediate implications:

- According to this proposed model, the black hole physical singularity is indeed unphysical, consequently it is plausible that black hole interiors consist of other cosmologies, and thus that our own cosmology may be identical to a black hole's interior.

- All the cosmological information is holographically embedded at its surface, and thus the closed region considered must expand with time at all times. Black holes *do not* shrink.

4. Conclusions

This chapter proposes the principle of vacuum diagram loop divergence treatment by analytic continuation (what may be referred to as the principle of analyticity) as a method for developing a tentative intuition on how to treat these vacuum diagram loop divergences in general. It is proposed that the virtual quantization is an inherent physical property due to periodic boundary conditions, and thus may exist independently of the presence of a Casimir cavity and can only be manipulated in magnitude by it. It is shown that by using this proposed physical principle, that it is possible to associate a physical value to the desired vacuum diagram Feynman loop integral, which would be identical to its physical value. The said proposed physical principle is referenced [10] to its application in the conformally flat dS case, which seems as far as the author of this chapter understands to be internally self-consistent for all inertial reference frames. It remains unclear whether or not it is covariant in general. Some immediate and simultaneous implications are restated for the sake of clarity and completeness. Some methods of error and falsification are then discussed, and concrete predictions stated.

Conflict of interest

The author declares no conflict of interest.

Availability of data and materials

No new data was generated during this study.

Abbreviations

dS	de-Sitter
vs.	versus
i.e.	that is
QFT	Quantum field theory
SI	System international
WLOG	Without loss of generality
&	and

Nomenclature

EOS	Equation of state
EOM	Equation of motion
default	magnitude without external manipulation

A. Appendix A

Here some quick derivations in Ref. to [10] are shown. The law of energy conservation of the system considered is

$$dQ = TdS + pdV = 0 \tag{13}$$

Note that the internal energy $dU = TdS$ does not need to originate from the black hole mass due to the extra term, that is. $TdS \neq dM$; hence, it is possible to avoid evaporation. Where the Hawking temperature T and the Bekenstein entropy S are given by [17].

$$T = \frac{\hbar c^3}{8\pi kGM} \tag{14}$$

$$S = \frac{k\pi R^2}{l_p^2} \tag{15}$$

Where l_p is the Planck length. Using the negative pressure up to a geometrical proportionality constant expected to be of order $O(-1)$

$$p_{dS} \propto -\frac{\hbar^2 c^6}{G} \tag{16}$$

And solving (Eq. (13)) for a sphere of radius R yields two global nonzero minima

$$M^2 \propto \left(\frac{c}{\hbar G}\right)^2 \tag{17}$$

Presumably corresponding to the matter vs. antimatter solutions.

Finally, the equivalence principle combined with the Friedmann equations [18] imply

$$g = a_{dS} = \sqrt{\frac{\Lambda_{dS}}{3}}c^2 \propto \hbar c^3 \tag{18}$$

which may be solved for a rotating massive body to give

$$v^4 \propto \hbar G c^3 M \tag{19}$$

Note that it is possible to re-derive (Eq. (17)) by setting $v = c$ up to a geometrical proportionality constant expected to be of $O(-1)$ independently of the usage of holography (Eq. (15)).

Author details

Adrian C. Eide
Independent Researcher, Oslo, Norway

*Address all correspondence to: adrianntnu@gmail.com

References

[1] Bekenstein JD. Black holes and entropy. Physical Review D. 1973;**7**(8): 2333-2346. DOI: 10.1103/PhysRevD.7.2333

[2] Hawking S. Black hole explosions? Nature. 1974;**248**:30-31. DOI: 10.1038/248030a0

[3] Calmet X, Hsu SDHA. Brief history of Hawking's information paradox. Europhysics Letters. 2022;**139**(4):49001 (1-5). DOI: 10.1209/0295-5075/ac81e8

[4] Davies PCW. Scalar production in Schwarzschild and Rindler metrics. Journal of Physics A: Mathematical and General. 1975;**8**(4):609. DOI: 10.1088/0305-4470/8/4/022

[5] Unruh WG. Notes on black-hole evaporation. Physical Review D. 1976;**14**(4):870-892. DOI: 10.1103/PhysRevD.14.870

[6] Veneziano G. Construction of a crossing-symmetric, Regge-behaved amplitude for linearly rising trajectories. Nuovo Cimento A. 1968;**1965-1970**(57): 190-197. DOI: 10.1007/BF02824451

[7] D'Hoker E, Phong DH. The box graph In superstring theory. Nuclear Physics. 1995;**B440**:24-94. DOI: 10.1016/0550-3213%2894%2900526-K

[8] Lamoreaux SK. The Casimir force: Background, experiments, and applications. Reports on Progress in Physics. 2004;**68**(1):201. DOI: 10.1088/0034-4885/68/1/R04

[9] Mohideen U. And Roy, Anushree, precision measurement of the Casimir force from 0.1 to 0.9 μ m. Physical Review Letters. 1998;**81**(21): 4549-4552. DOI: 10.1103/PhysRevLett.81.4549

[10] Eide AC. On virtual scalar fields in a conformally flat FLRW spacetime. Journal of Mathematical Techniques and Computational Mathematics. 2022;**1**(2): 129-132. DOI: 10.33140/JMTCM.01.02.07

[11] Kachelriess M. Quantum Fields: From the Hubble to the Planck Scale. Oxford: Oxford University Press; 2018. pp. 186-187

[12] Kachelriess M. Quantum Fields: From the Hubble to the Planck Scale. Oxford: Oxford University Press; 2018. pp. 47-49

[13] Aghanim N, Akrami Y, Ashdown M, Aumont J, Baccigalupi C, Ballardini M, et al. Planck 2018 results. VI. Cosmological Parameters. arXiv. 2020;**641**:17 (Eq. 15)

[14] McGaugh SS et al. The baryonic Tully-fisher relation. ApJ. 2000;**533**(2): L99. DOI: 10.1086/312628

[15] Hawking S. Properties of Expanding Universes [Thesis]. Cambridge: Cambridge Books; 1966. pp. 114-116. DOI: 10.17863/CAM.11283

[16] Eide AC. On the necessity of the existence of the cosmological scales. Journal of Mathematical Techniques and Computational Mathematics. 2022;**1**(3): 184. DOI: 10.33140/JMTCM.01.03.03

[17] Hartle JB. Gravity an Introduction to Einstein's General Relativity. Boston: Addision Wesley (Pearson Education); 2003. pp. 293-294 (Eq. 13.13 and Eq. 13.18)

[18] Hartle JB. Gravity an Introduction to Einstein's General Relativity. Boston: Addision Wesley (Pearson Education); 2003. p. 379 (Eq. 18.40)

Chapter 2

Calculations of Flows with Deflagration Appearance in Channels with Obstacles

Sergey Martyushov

Abstract

Many researches devoted to deflagration appearance in hydrogen-air mixes and transition it to detonation. This is connected with the problem of detonation hydrogen engine construction. A new way of detonation engine construction connected with using different fuel mixes: $CO + H_2$ or kerosene-hydrogen mixes. In these cases, it seems to be preferable for mathematical modeling to use fool system of reactions for all components and radicals. Using of fool system of kinetic equation allows one to determine moment of deflagration initiation and transition it to detonation. In laboratory experiments deflagration initiation appears as a result of energy and temperature grows by successive triggering of electric discharges or near obstacles in channels. In many papers numerically investigated flows of reactive gas mixes in channels with obstacles or initiation of deflagration via hot spot as a model to electric discharges. In this chapter numerically investigated flows of reactive gas mixes in channels with obstacles with the purpose to define conditions of deflagration initiation.

Keywords: transition from deflagration to detonation, numerical method for stiff system of differential equation decision, multistage chemical reactions, quasi-stationary concentration of radicals, branching chain reaction theory

1. Introduction

Several last decades idea of detonation engine was in center of attention of researchers. Detonation fuel cycle is more energetic preferable than used in aviation and rocket engine constructions Briton cycle. So, simplicity of construction and energetic effectiveness make development of detonation engine constructions very perspective.

Detonation engine construction can be used in electricity if not paid attention to size and weight of engine. An example of such energetic construction was made in Bussing [1].

During the last three decades, some experimental laboratory constructions were made [2–4] for investigation of engine constructions, and works on mixing methane-air, methane-oxygen, and kerosene-air as fuels. All these fuel mixes have low detonation possibility, which demands additional energetic income for detonation initiation. This initiation can be achieved by electric discharges [5] or by specification of region inside engine: channels with obstacles, ring or U-tube form of the channel [6], focusing of pulse jet inside sphere-shape resonator [7] or spin detonation engine, in which detonation wave propagates inside axis symmetrical region in radial direction [8].

Progress in decision of problem of detonation engine construction partly consists of numerical simulation of gas flow inside the engine. This numerical simulation demands development of sophisticated mathematical models and numerical methods of high order of accuracy.

In the first period simplified model of chemical reactions of Levin et al. [9] was used, in papers of Fujiwara [10] for example. Nowadays various full systems of chemical reactions are used, which consist of many reactions ([11] for example). In the second section of this chapter mathematical model for numerical simulation of reactive gas mixes flows is described. Also in this section numerical method of solving system of gas dynamic equations for an arbitrary number of mixed components is introduced. This numerical method is based on a variant of Shakravarthy-Osher non-linear TVD (total variation diminishing) difference scheme of third order of accuracy [12].

In the system of gas dynamics (2) exist source term of speeds of changing mix components concentrations as result of chemical reactions. Values of this term determine growth of internal energy and temperature, so defining of this term is essential part of mathematical model and numerical method. Appearance of deflagration and transition from slow deflagration to detonation in reactive gas mixes flows depend on how intensive are chemical reactions in flow.

In the third section of this chapter mathematical model of a system of ordinary differential kinetic equations for the concentration of gas mix components is described. Numerical solutions of this system of equations are discussed.

The process of detonation appearance in hydrogen-air mixes can be treated as a transition from slow chemical reactions to fast branching chain reactions in hydrogen-air (or other components) mixes. The theory of these reactions was developed by Semenov [13] (see also Denisov et al. [14]). Now this approach intensively developed in the papers of some authors: Saeid et al. [15], Liu et al. [16].

2. Numerical simulation of reactive gas mixes flows

For numerical simulation of reactive gas mixes flows the system of equations of an ideal gas for two-dimensional flows (with source terms which are velocities of changing gas mix components via chemical reaction) can be written in integral form for finite volume cell:

$$d/dt \int_V QdV + \oint_S nFdS + \Phi = 0 \qquad (1)$$

where $Q = \left(\rho, \vec{m}, \rho e, \rho c_i\right), i = 1, \dots n$, is vector of m conservative unknown, n is number of mix components, $\vec{m} = (\rho u, \rho v)$ is vector of impulse, and $c_i = \rho_i/\rho$ are mass concentrations of mix components (where i = 1, ... , n is number of mix component). The source term has the form:

$$\Phi = (0, 0, 0, 0, d\rho c_i/dt_{chem}). \tag{2}$$

Tensor of flows is equal to: $\tilde{F} = \left(\vec{m}, \left(\vec{m} \cdot \vec{m}\right)/\rho + P\tilde{I}, \vec{m}(e+P)/\rho, \vec{m}c_i\right)$.

For implementation non-linear TVD difference scheme, it is necessary to define flows on the border of finite volume cell on the basis of some approximate Riemann solvers. In this chapter those approximate Riemann solvers where defined (initially find in Martyushov [17]) for arbitrary number of gas mix components on the basis of Roe-Pike method, explanation of which can be found, for example, in Toro [18]. Flows on the border of finite volume cell for approximate Riemann solvers are:

$$F_L + \sum_{\tilde{\lambda}_k \le 0} \Delta_{i+1/2} W_k \tilde{\lambda}_k r_k = F_R + \sum_{\tilde{\lambda}_k \ge 0} \Delta_{i+1/2} W_k \tilde{\lambda}_k r_k \;\; \Delta F = \sum_{k=1}^{m} \Delta_{i+1/2} W_k \tilde{\lambda}_k r_k, \tag{3}$$

where ΔW_k intensity of characteristic wave. For calculation of flow on the bound of control volume we have the next relations:

$$F_{i+1/2} = \frac{1}{2}(F_L + F_R) - \frac{1}{2}\sum_{k=1}^{m} \Delta_{i+1/2} W_k |\tilde{\lambda}_k| r_k \tag{4}$$

where r_k I_k are right and left eigen vectors of Jacobian matrix $A(Q) = \partial F/\partial Q$. $\Delta W = L\Delta Q$. For calculation of ΔW it is sufficient to use this equality, where $\Delta Q = (\Delta\rho, \Delta(\rho U), \Delta(\rho V), \Delta E, \Delta(\rho c_1), \dots \Delta(\rho c_n))^T, i = 1, n$. where right eigen vectors are:

$$\begin{aligned}
r_1 &= (0, 0, 1, V, 0, \dots, 0)^T, r_2 = (1, U, V, \omega, 0, \dots, 0)^T, r_3 = (1, U+a, V, H+Ua, c_1, \dots, c_n)^T, \\
r_4 &= (1, U-a, V, H-Ua, c_1, \dots, c_n)^T, r_5 = (0, 0, 0, h_1, 1, 0, \dots, 0)^T, \\
r_6 &= (0, 0, 0, h_2, 0, 1, 0, \dots, 0)^T, r_n = (0, 0, 0, h_n, 0, 0, \dots, 1)^T.
\end{aligned} \tag{5}$$

The next eigen values where chosen: $\lambda = (U, U, U+a, U-a, U, \dots, U)$.

Denoting $\Delta W = (\alpha_1, \alpha_2, \alpha_3, \alpha_4, \alpha_5, \dots, \alpha_n)$ for finding $\Delta W = L\Delta Q$ we can solve system of equation for finding $\Delta WR = \Delta Q$:

$$\begin{aligned}
&\alpha_2 + \alpha_3 + \alpha_4 = \Delta\rho \\
&U\alpha_2 + (U+a)\alpha_3 + (U-a)\alpha_4 = \Delta(\rho U) \\
&\alpha_1 + V\alpha_2 + V\alpha_3 + V\alpha_4 = \Delta(\rho V) \\
&V\alpha_1 + \omega\alpha_2 + (H+Ua)\alpha_3 + (H-Ua)\alpha_4 + \sum_{i=1}^{n} \alpha_6 h_i = \Delta(E) \\
&c_i\alpha_3 + c_i\alpha_4 + \alpha_i = \Delta(\rho c_i), i = 1, n.
\end{aligned} \tag{6}$$

System (6) can be solved by consequent excluding of unknowns:

$$
\begin{aligned}
\alpha_2 &= \left(\Delta\rho \left(H - U^2 - \sum_{i=1}^{n} c_i h_i \right) + \Delta(\rho U)U + \sum_{i=1}^{n} h_i \Delta(\rho c_i) - \overline{E} \right) / \omega \\
\alpha_4 &= ((U + a)\Delta\rho - \Delta(\rho U) - a\alpha_2)/2a \\
\alpha_3 &= (-(U - a)\Delta\rho + \Delta(\rho U) - a\alpha_2)/2a \\
\alpha_1 &= \Delta(\rho V) - V\Delta\rho \\
\alpha_{i+4} &= \Delta(\rho c_i) - c_i(\Delta\rho - \alpha_2), i = 1, n \\
\overline{E} &= \Delta E - V(\Delta(\rho V) - V\Delta\rho).
\end{aligned} \tag{7}
$$

The TVD difference scheme of Chacravarthy-Osher [12] was used for solving system (1). This scheme is one of third order of accuracy and can be written in such form (for flow on the border of finite volume in (4)):

Preliminary step:

$$
\alpha^i_{1,m+1/2} = l^i_{m+1/2}(U_m - U_{m-1}); \alpha^i_{2,m+1/2} = l^i_{m+1/2}(U_{m+1} - U_m); \alpha^i_{3,m+1/2} = l^i_{m+1/2}(U_{m+2} - U_{m+1});
$$

$$
\lambda^{i+}_{m+1/2} = \begin{cases} \lambda^i_{m+1/2}, .\lambda^i_{m+1/2} > 0 \\ 0, .\lambda^i_{m+1/2} < 0 \end{cases}, \quad \lambda^{i-}_{m+1/2} = \begin{cases} \lambda^i_{m+1/2}, .\lambda^i_{m+1/2} < 0 \\ 0, .\lambda^i_{m+1/2} > 0 \end{cases}; \tag{8}
$$

$$
\overline{\alpha}^i_{1,m+1/2} = \min\bmod\left\{\alpha^i_{1,m+1/2}, b\alpha^i_{2,m+1/2}\right\}; \tilde{\alpha}^i_{2,m+1/2} = \min\bmod\left\{\alpha^i_{2,m+1/2}, b\alpha^i_{1,m+1/2}\right\};
$$

$$
\overline{\alpha}^i_{2,m+1/2} = \min\bmod\left\{\alpha^i_{2,m+1/2}, b\alpha^i_{3,m+1/2}\right\}; \tilde{\alpha}^i_{3,m+1/2} = \min\bmod\left\{\alpha^i_{3,m+1/2}, b\alpha^i_{2,m+1/2}\right\}
$$

where $\min\bmod(x, y) = \operatorname{sgn}(x)\max[0, \min(|x|, y\operatorname{sgn}(x)]$.

Main step:

$$
\begin{aligned}
F_{m+1/2} = H_{m+1/2} &+ \sum_i \left(\frac{1+\delta}{4} \tilde{\alpha}^i_{1,m+1/2} + \frac{1-\delta}{4} \overline{\alpha}^i_{2,m+1/2} \right) \lambda^{i+}_{m+1/2} r^i_{m+1/2} \\
&- \sum_i \left(\frac{1+\delta}{4} \overline{\alpha}^i_{2,m+1/2} + \frac{1-\delta}{4} \tilde{\alpha}^i_{3,m+1/2} \right) \lambda^{i-}_{m+1/2} r^i_{m+1/2}
\end{aligned} \tag{9}
$$

The first term in (9) is:

$$
H_{m+1/2} = \frac{1}{2}[F(Q_{m+1}) + F(Q_m)] - \frac{1}{2}\sum_i \left(\lambda^{i+}_{m+1/2} - \lambda^{i-}_{m+1/2} \right) \alpha^i_{2,m+1/2} r^i_{m+1/2} \tag{10}
$$

Parameter $b = (3 - \delta)/(1 - \delta)$, and parameter δ determine order of approximation of the scheme. Meaning δ = 1/3 gives to scheme third order of approximation.

Time approximation was made on the basis of Runge-Kutta scheme of fourth order of accuracy.

Implementation of the Roe-Pike method for calculation of flows of reactive gas mixes flows was used by author in Martyushov [17]. Modification of numerical method [17] in this chapter consists of using meaning of parameter δ = 1. This meaning of δ preserve pure upwind variant of this scheme. This variant of scheme made it possible to avoid oscillations of values of radicals components concentration in regions of deflagration appearance.

The velocity of gas mix in gas dynamic flows is of order of sound speed 300 m/s in air. Pressure in the CI dimension system is of 10^5 pascal. For the aim of minimizing truncation errors procedure of transition to non-dimensional unknowns was provided. Non- dimensional gas dynamic values were used: $P' = P/\left(\rho_0 c_0^2\right), \rho' = \rho, \vec{V}' = \vec{V}/c_0^2, T' = T/c_0^2, t' = t/c_0$—time of process is of sec $\times 10^{-5}$ order.

For this reason, in Section 5 of this chapter physical parameters in results have dimension only temperature is in Kelvin degrees (pressure can be found from equation of state for ideal gas mix), time of process is of order sec $\times 10^{-5}$ and concentration of components are measured in percent of density or molar units.

3. Kinetic model

For process of deflagration in reactive gas mixes the most important term in system (1) is $d\rho c_i/dt_{chem}$ (in source tern Φ) which determine, appearance of deflagration and transitions it to detonation, and as a result intensive growth of energy and temperature. The algorithm for calculation of this term will be described in this section of the chapter.

Equations of chemical reactions can be presented as follows:

$$\sum_{i=1}^{n} \alpha_{ij} A_i = \sum_{i=1}^{n} \beta_{ij} B_i, j = 1, \dots, M \tag{11}$$

where n is number of components of the mix and M *is* number of reactions, coefficients α_{ij}, β_{ij} are numbers of molecules (or moll) of mix components in direct and inverse reactions, A_i is reagents and B_i is products of direct reactions. Arrhenius low was used for calculating speeds of changing of mix components concentration c_i:

$$\frac{dc_i}{dt} = \sum_{j=1}^{M} \left(\beta_{ij} - \alpha_{ij}\right) w_j(c, T), \tag{12}$$

$$w_j(c, T) = k_f(T) \prod_{i=1}^{n} c_i^{\alpha_{ij}} - k_b(T) \prod_{i=1}^{n} c_i^{\beta_{ij}}, \tag{13}$$

$$k_{f,b} = A_{f,b} T^{l_{f,b}} \exp\left(-E_{f,b}/RT\right)), \tag{14}$$

where meanings of α_{ij}, β_{ij} are taken from (11). In the present chapter gas mix of nine component: H_2, O_2, H, O, H_2O, OH, HO_2, H_2O_2, N_2 was treated. The next 11 reactions were chosen:

Two algorithms were used for numerical solving of system (12)–(14). The first one was solving of fool system of stiff ODE (12)–(14) on the basis of implicit numerical Gear method. Constants of reactions in (12)–(14) were taken from Ibragimova et al. [19]. The other meanings of this constant can be found in Refs. [11, 14].

The model problem of initiation of deflagration as a result of sudden temperature increase in hot spot in closed volume was numerically simulated. In **Figure 1(a)** and **(b)** (initiation of deflagration as result of temperature meaning increasing to 2.4 and 2.7 times from initial atmospheric one (293 K degree) in part of closed volume), graphics of molar concentration of mix components are drawn,

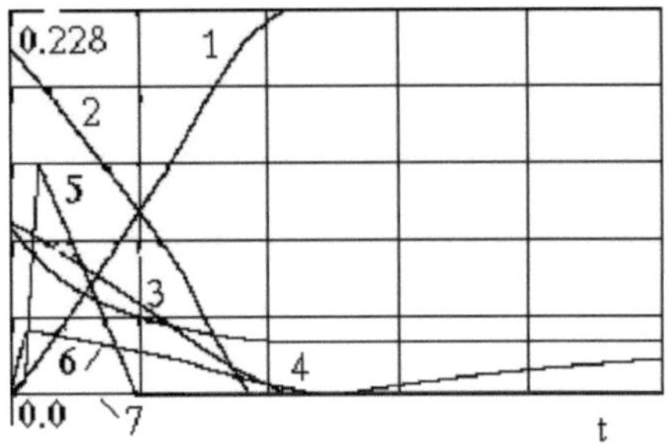

(a)

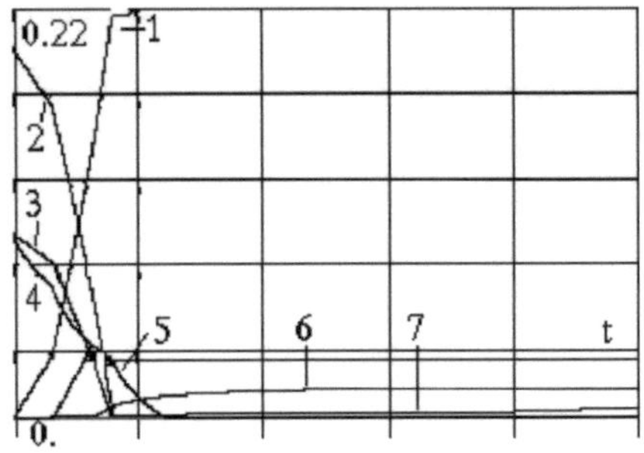

(b)

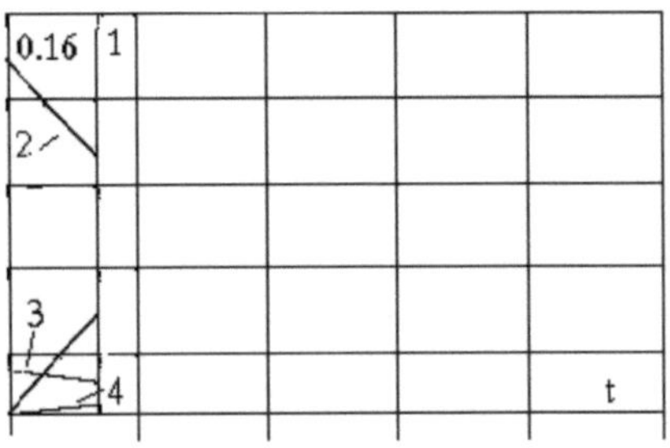

(c)

Figure 1.
(a)–(c) Graphics of molar concentrations of mixed components from time (time is measured in seconds, meanings varies from 1 to 30, and concentrations measured in part of mass units).

consequently: line 1 is graphic of H_2O molar concentration, line 2 is graphic of H_2 molar concentration, *line* 3 is graphic of O_2, line 4 (line up to the mark "4") is graphic of $1/T$ (inverse to temperature), line 5 is graphic of H_2O_2 molar concentration, line 6 is graphic of H molar concentration, and line 7 is graphic of HO_2 molar concentration (graphics 5–7 multiplied by 10^2). On x-axes is time in seconds, and on y-axes is concentration of components in unity of part of mixed mass. In **Figure 1(b)** graphics 1–5 have the same meanings, line 6 is graphic of HO_2, and line 7 is graphic of OH molar concentration (graphics 5–7 multiplied by 10^2).

Intensive changes of O_2 and H_2 (that means deflagration initiation) begin after grows of H_2O_2 value, so that means that the influence of radical H_2O_2 appearance is important just in the same degree as influence of radical H appearance for initiation of deflagration.

Idea of the second calculation algorithm for the same problem is the next [13, 14]. In process of deflagration appearance in hydrogen-air gas mix sudden explosion appears after long period of induction. In this induction period concentrations of radicals H, O, HO_2, H_2O_2, and OH grows. This explosion mechanism is branching chain reactions. Theory of branching chain reactions was introduced by Semenov [13]. In this theory system of two differential equations for concentration of H and H_2O_2 (in Semenov [13] only one equation for H) is solving separately, concentration of radicals H, O, OH, and HO_2 are found from algebraic relation from assumption of "quasi-stationary" concentration, and for "large unknowns" system of three differential equations is solved with bigger time step. System of two differential equations for concentration of H and H_2O_2 take s form:

$$d\,[H]/dt = 2k_0\,[H_2]\,[O_2] + \Phi\,[H] – k_7\,[H]^2$$
$$\Phi = 2k_2\,[O_2] - k_5\,[O_2] – k_6\,[H_2O] – k_{11}\,[H_2O_2]. \quad (15)$$
$$d[H_2O_2]/dt = k_8\,[HO_2]^2 - k_9\,[H_2O_2]\,[M] + k_{10}\,[OH]^2\,[M] - k_9\,[H_2O_2]\,[H].$$

Molar concentrations of "quasi -stationary" components [O], $[HO_2]$, and [OH] can be found in algebraic equations:

$$\begin{aligned}
&[O] = [H](k_2\,[O_2])/(k_3\,[H_2]);\\
&[OH] = (2[O_2][H_2]k_0 + k_6\,[H_2O][H] + 2\,k_9\,[H_2O_2]\,[M]\\
&+k_{11}[H_2O_2][H])(k_1\,[H_2] + 2k_{10}\,[M];\\
&[HO_2]^2 = k_5\,[H]\,[O_2]\,[M]/(2\,k_8).
\end{aligned} \quad (16)$$

The other components of the mix are found from equations for the rest unknowns of system (12)–(14).

The same model problem was numerically simulated using branching chain reaction theory (15) and (16).

Results of calculation 0n the basis of this algorithm are shown in **Figure 1c**, namely graphics of mass concentration of components (initial temperature meaning is increasing to 2.5 times from initial atmospheric one (293 K degree) in part of closed volume), line 1 is graphic of H_2O mass concentration, line 2 is graphic of H_2 mass concentration, line 3 is graphic of O_2 and line 4 is graphic of H_2O_2 multiplied by 10^2.

Calculations of systems of ODE (12)–(14) and (15)–(16) are provided by Goer difference scheme with time scale of order sec. Calculation of system of gas dynamic (4) by algorithm (9) provided with time scale of order $\sec \times 10^{-5}$. For reason of different time steps in whole algorithm (gas dynamic plus kinetic), it demands to provide 20 gas dynamic steps for one chemical step.

4. Construction of calculation grids

Curvilinear structured grids, used in numerical simulation of this chapter, were constructed by algorithm of author [20] and consist of solution of system of PDE equation of parabolic type. Construction of such grids is not a simple problem, sometimes calculation grid, constructed absolutely writes theoretically, produces oscillations, and wrong results in gas dynamics calculation. Examples of curvilinear grids for axis symmetrical channels with obstacles are shown in **Figure 2(a)–(c)**.

5. Numerical simulation of gas mixes flows with deflagration

Numerical simulations of two-dimensional axis symmetrical flows of hydrogen-air mixes with deflagration were provided for some configurations of axis symmetrical channels with obstacles.

Due to high speed of gas dynamics flows and chemical reactions for mathematical model (1) normalizing performed similar to ones for Reynolds number definition for viscous liquid flows performed. The next characteristic values were used for normalizing. So non-dimension meanings for time, linear scale, and physical parameters were used. On graphics lower only temperature was in Kelvin degree and concentration of components

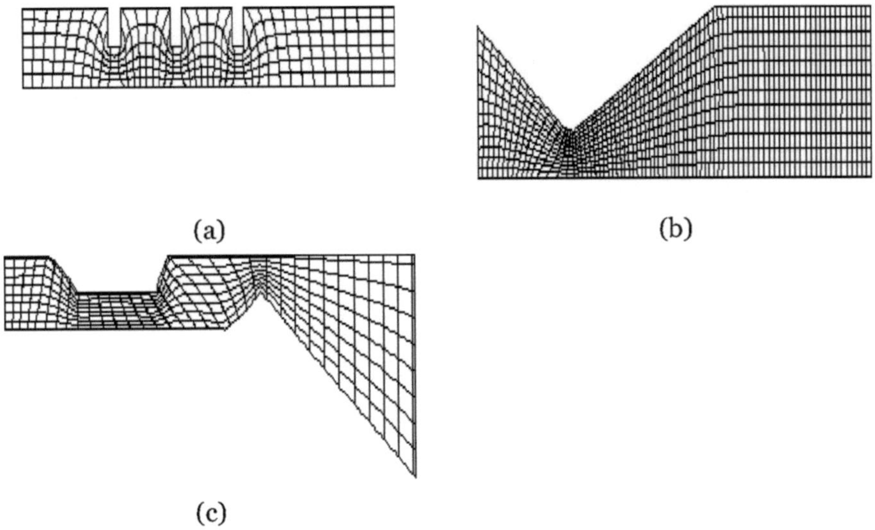

Figure 2.
(a)–(c) Calculation grids for axis symmetrical channels with obstacles, near which initiation of deflagration appears (every tenth coordinate line is drawn).

of mixes in molar units. For other physical parameters (include time scale and linear sizes of calculation region), non-dimension parameters were taken in the next form:

$$t' = t \cdot l/c_0, P' = P/c_0^2\rho_0, E' = E/c_0^2, \tag{17}$$

where ρ_0 is density of atmosphere gas, ${c_0}^2$ is square of atmosphere sound speed, and l is character size of calculation region. In non-dimension time scale calculation were provided for 3000–5000 time step (in non-dimension time units till 200–300 units).

Formulation of the mathematical problem for all geometry regions (**Figure 2(a)–(c)**) is the next. Initially calculation region was filled by hydrogen-air mix with a shock wave and the region after it near the left boundary of the region. On the left boundary of calculation regions boundary conditions with parameters of gas mixes behind the shock wave were established. On the top boundary of calculation region non-penetration conditions were used, on the bottom boundary conditions of axes of symmetry or non-penetration conditions were established. On the right boundary non-reflection conditions were used. In right part of the region before the shock wave meanings of gas dynamics parameters were atmospheric ones.

For all flows calculated in this section stoichiometric hydrogen-air composition of mix (20% of H_2, 10% of O_2, and 70% of N_2) was used in whole region with small (less than 2%) include of water as catalyst.

$H_2 + O_2 - k_0 - 2OH$	$H_2 + OH - k_1 - H + H_2O$	$H + O_2 - k_2 - O + OH$
$H_2 + O - k_3 - H + OH$	$HO_2 + M - k_5 - H + O_2 + M$	$H + H_2O - k_6 - H_2 + OH$
$2H + M - k_7 - H_2 + M$	$2HO_2 - k_8 - H_2O_2 + O_2$	$H_2O_2 + M - k_9 - 2OH + M$
$2OH + M - k_{10} - H_2O_2 + M$	$H + H_2O_2 - k_{11} - OH + H_2O$	

Table 1.
Chemical reactions (component M in reactions means some collision partner of reaction, k_i*—speed of appropriate direct reaction* k_f*).*

5.1 Flow in non-reflecting nozzle

Axis symmetrical channel with non-reflecting nozzle (calculation grid drawn in **Figure 2(b)**) initially filled with hydrogen-air mix with little amount of water (less than 2%, it involved as collision partner in reactions 5 and 7 of **Table 1**) with atmosphere meanings of gas dynamics values. At the initial moment shock wave of

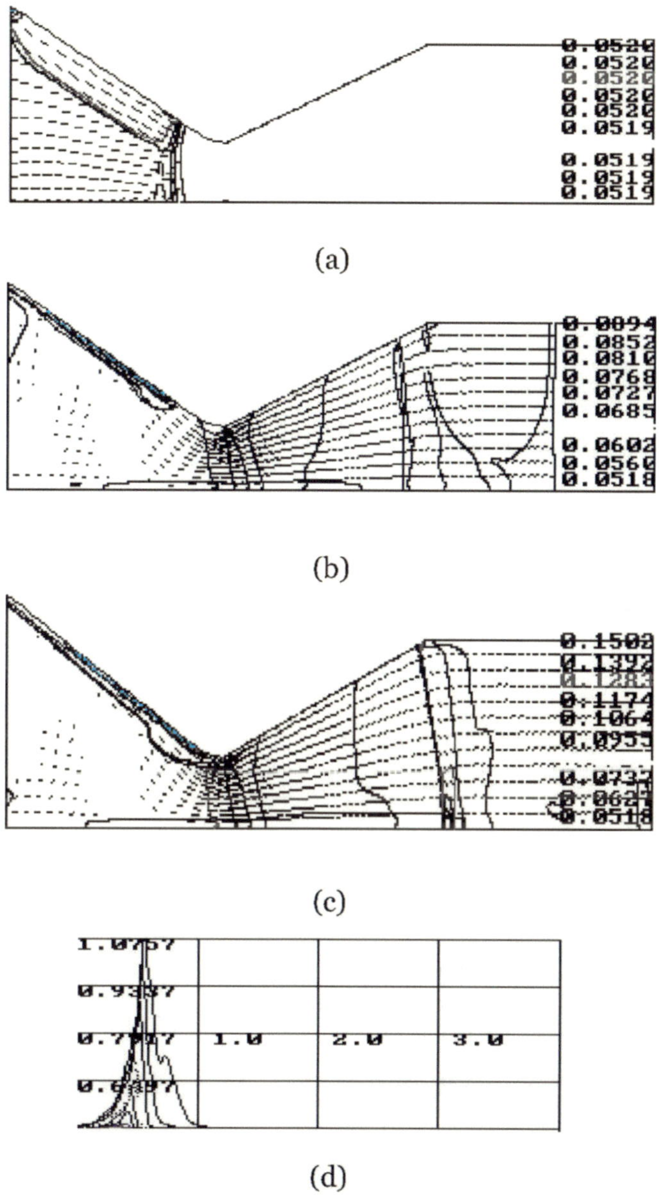

Figure 3.
(a)–(c) Vectors of velocity, level lines of temperature and in right number column corresponding to level lines meanings of concentration in percent of H_2O in consecutive time moments; (d) graphic of concentration of water along top boundary of the channel in consequent moments (along y-axis graphics of concentration in moll units, along x-axes is numbers of grid point in the x-direction).

intensity $M_{sh.w.}$ = 1.9 (Mach number of sh0ck wave is the relation of shock wave speed to sound speed before shock) began to move from the left side of the region.

During the spreading of shock wave on the top bound of the region (conical surface) deflagration of gas mix appears. On **Figure 3(a)–(c)** level lines of temperature and meanings of water concentration in percentage (in number column) in consequent time moments are drawn. Change of this concentration inside the flow (**Figure 3(c)**, from 5% to 15% of whole mass) demonstrates deflagration appearance. On **Figure 3(d)** graphics of water concentration along top boundary of the channel in consequent time moments are drawn (along y-axis concentration in percents of mass, along x-axes number of grid point in x-direction). Temperature of deflagration appearance approximately 700–800 K degree.

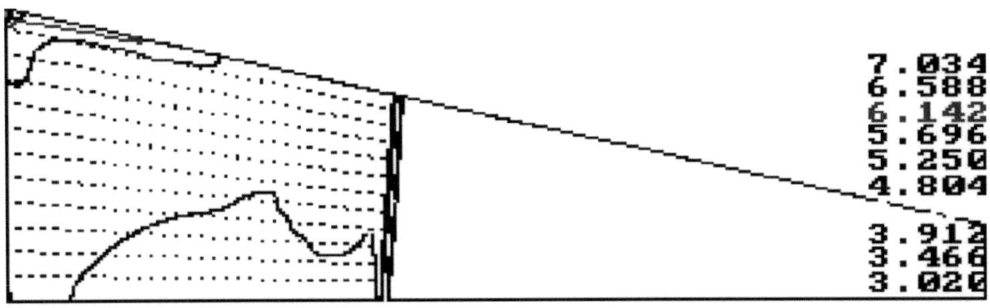

(a)

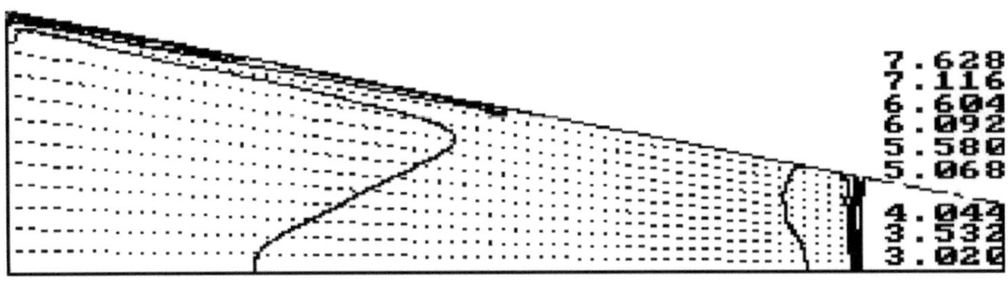

(b)

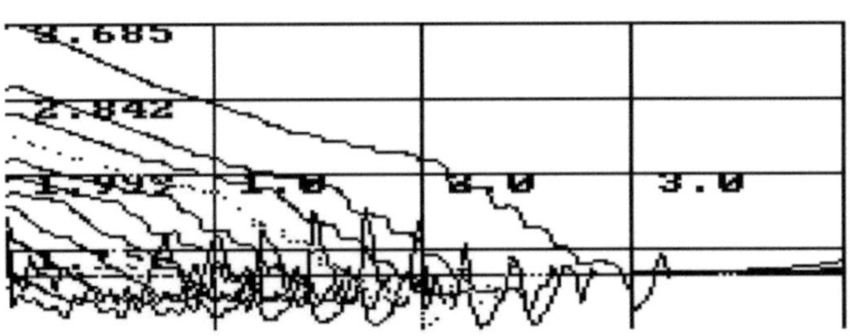

(c)

Figure 4.
(a) and (b) Vectors of velocity, level lines of temperature and in right number column corresponding to level lines meanings of temperature in Kelvin in two consecutive time moments; (c) graphics of molar concentration of water along top boundary of the channel in consequent time moments (along y-axis graphics of concentration in moll units, along x-axes is numbers of grid point in x-direction).

5.2 Flow in cone-form channel

Axis symmetrical calculation region is a channel between cone surface and cylinder. The shock wave of intensity $M_{sh.w.} = 3.1$ spreading from the left boundary of the region. There is no one point of compression of flow in this problem. Compression takes place along all top boundaries of the region and strengthens with time. In **Figure 4(a)** and **(b)** level lines of temperature and temperature meanings (in right number column) in two consequent time moments are drawn. In **Figure 4(c)**, graphics of concentration of water along top boundary of the channel in consequent time moments are drawn (along y-axis concentration in percents of whole mass, along x-axes number of grid point in x-direction).

5.3 Flow in complex form channel with obstacles

Numerical simulation of flows with deflagration appearance in axis-symmetric channels of complex form with obstacles was provided. Curvilinear structural grids for region of channel were constructed on the basis of algorithm [20] (**Figure 2(c)**). In **Figure 5(a)** and **(b)** level lines of temperature and meanings of molecular hydrogen in percents of mass concentration multiply to 10^3 (in right number column) in two consequent moments are drawn. Areas of concentration of level lines correspond to fronts of deflagration waves.

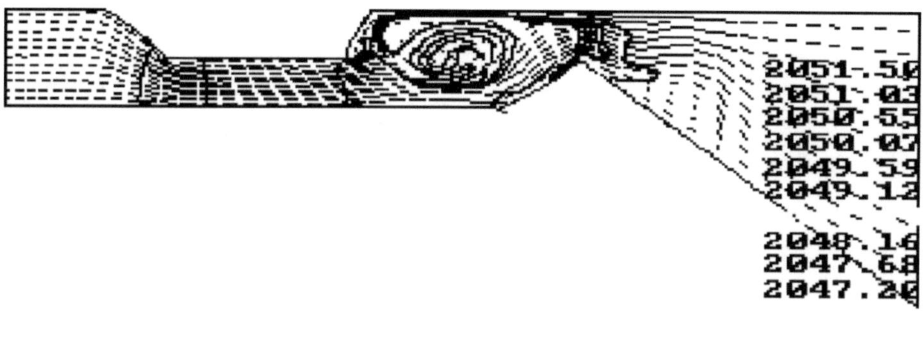

(a)

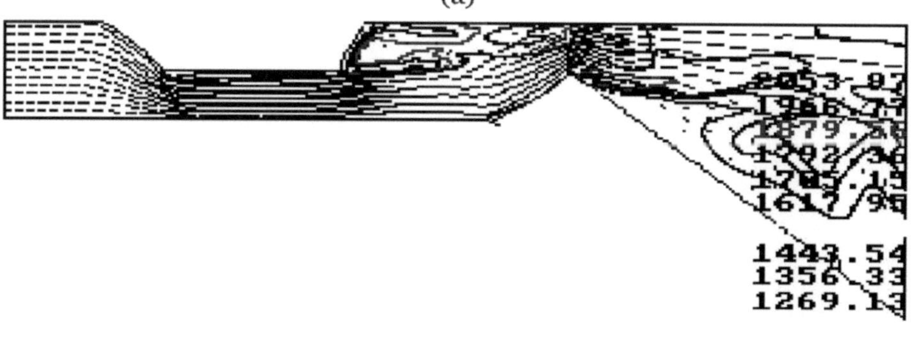

(b)

Figure 5.
(a) and (b) Vectors of velocity, level lines of temperature and in write column corresponding to level lines meanings of molar concentration of H_2 in percentage multiplied by 10^3 inside the axis-symmetric channel in consecutive time moments are drawn.

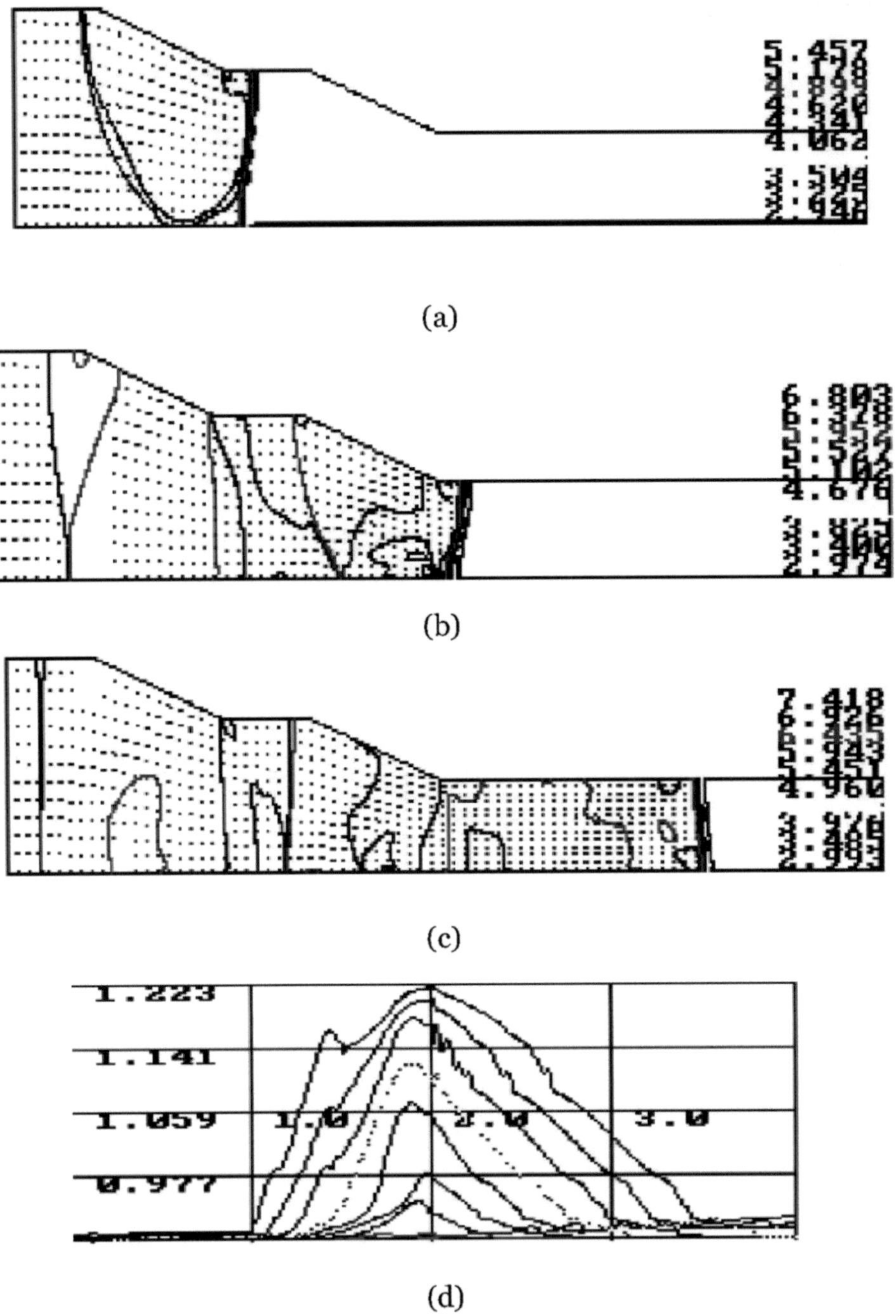

Figure 6.
(a)–(c) Vectors of velocity, level lines of temperature and in right column corresponding to level lines meanings of temperature in Kelvin in consecutive three moments; (d) graphic of molar concentration of water along top boundary of the channel in consequent time moments (along y-axis concentration in moll units, along x-axes is numbers of grid point in x-direction).

5.4 Flow in channel form which consist of combination of cylinders and cones

The axis symmetrical calculation region consists of combination of cylinders and cones. The shock wave of intensity $M_{sh.w.} = 2.7$ spreading from the left boundary of the region. Deflagration appears at the boundary point between second cone and second cylinder. In **Figure 6(a)–(c)** level lines of temperature and meanings of temperature in Kelvin degree (in right column) in three consequent moments are drawn. In **Figure 6(d)**, graphics of concentration of water along top boundary of the channel in consequent moments are drawn (along y-axis concentration in molar units, along x-axes is numbers of grid point in x-direction).

5.5 Flow in cylinder with obstacles

The calculation region (calculation grid is drawn in **Figure 1(a)**) consists of cylinder with three obstacles. The shock wave of initial intensity $M_{sh.w.} = 2.2$ moves from the left boundary of the region. Deflagration appears at the obstacles and, later near axes of symmetry. In **Figure 7(a)–(d)** level lines of temperature and water concentration (at the same picture) in four consequent moments are drawn. In **Figure 7(e)**, graphics of molar concentration of water along ax of symmetry of the channel in consequent time moments are drawn (along y-axis concentration of water in moll units, along x-axes number of grid point in x-direction).

6. Conclusions

In the chapter algorithm of calculation flows of reactive gas mixes with arbitrary number of component was provided. This algorithm consists of modification of one, developed in Martyushov [17] and based on pure upwind variant of Chakravarthy-Osher difference scheme. This modification allows to avoid oscillations of values of radicals concentrations in regions of deflagration appearance during calculations of hydrogen-air mixes flows.

Calculations of flows with the initiation of deflagration in hydrogen-air mixes in some geometries of channels with obstacles by this algorithm modification were provided.

For getting solution of system of kinetic equations as part of gas dynamic calculation two algorithms were used: Algorithm of solution of fool system of kinetic equation for multistage hydrogen-air reaction, and algorithm of separate solution of two parts of system of kinetic equation with different size of time step based on Semenov's theory of branching chain reaction.

Structured curvilinear calculation grids for calculation performed were constructed by author's algorithm.

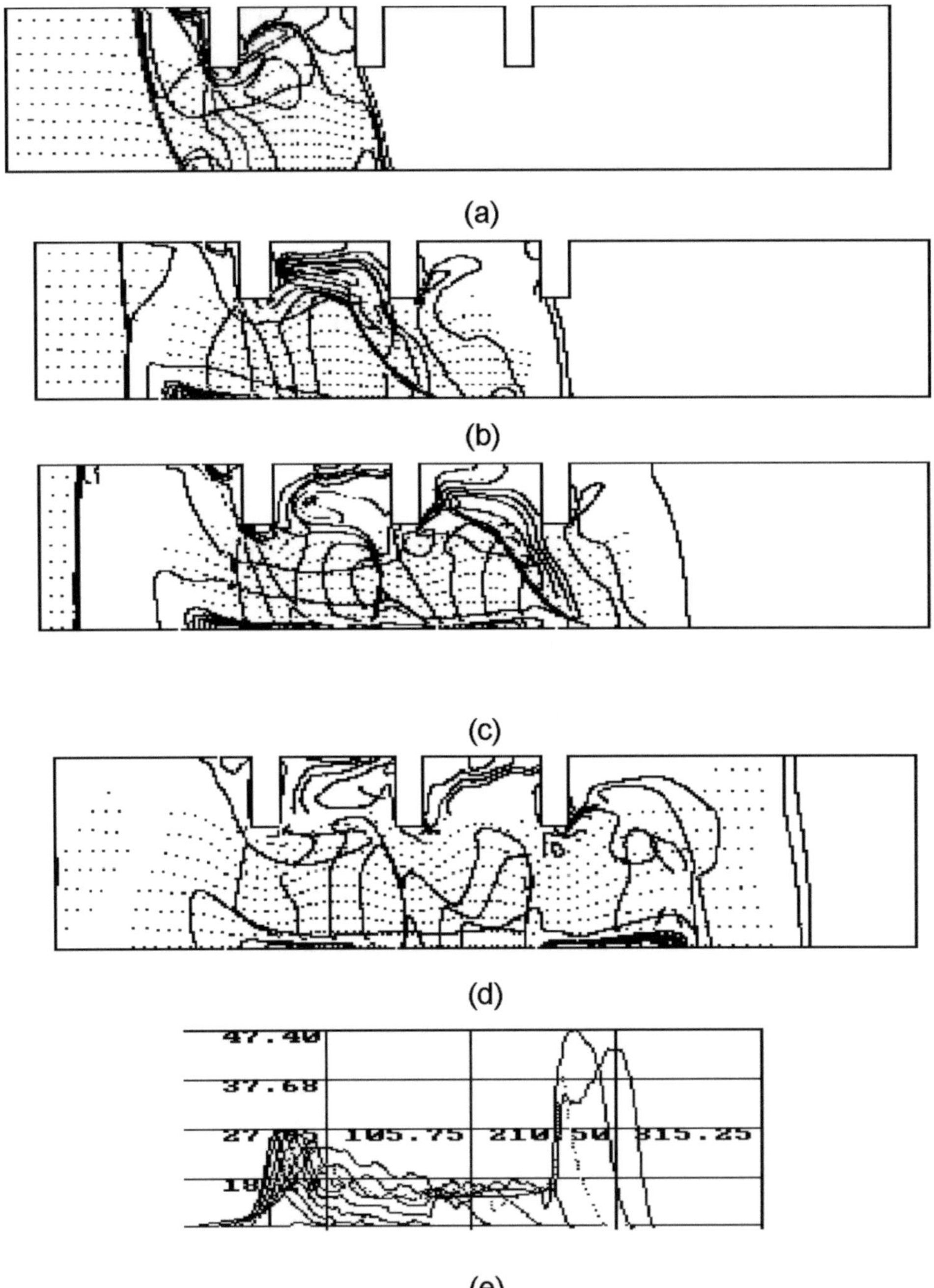

Figure 7.
(a)–(d) Vectors of velocity, level lines of temperature and water concentration (on the same picture); on (e) graphics of concentration of water along the ax of symmetry of the channel in consequent time moments are drawn (along y-axis concentration in moll units, along x-axes is numbers of grid point in x-direction).

Author details

Sergey Martyushov
Moscow Aviation Institute—National Research University, Moscow, Russian Federation

*Address all correspondence to: martyush@mail.ru

References

[1] Bussing T. US Patent. № 6.062.018. Date of Patent: May 16, 2000

[2] Roy GD, Frolov SM, Borisov A, Netzer D. Pulse detonation propulsion : Challenges, current status and future perspective. Progress in Energy and Combustion Science. 2004;**30**(6): 545-672

[3] Brophy SM, Netzer DW, Sinibaldi J, Johnson R. Detonation of JP-10 aerosol for pulse detonation application. In: Roy G, Frolov S, Netzer D, Borisov A, editors. High-Speed Deflagration and Detonation: Fundamental Control. Moscow: ELEX KM Pub; 2001. pp. 207-222

[4] Snauer F, Stutrud j., Bradley R., Katta V., Hoke j. Detonation studies and performance results for a research pulse detonation engine. In: Roy G, Frolov C, Santoro R, Tsyganov S, editors. Confined Detonations and Pulse Detonation Engines. Moscow: TORUS-PRESS; 2003. pp. 287-302

[5] Frolov S, Basevich VY, Aksenov VS, Polikhov SA. Initiation of spray detonation by successive triggering of electric discharges. Reports of Russian Academy of Sciences. 2004;**394**(4): 503-505

[6] Frolov S, Aksenov VS, Shamshin IO. Shock wave and detonation propagation trough U-bend tube. Proceedings of the Combustion Institute. 2007;**31**:2421-2428

[7] Levin VA, Nechaev YN, Tarasov AI. In: Roy G, editor. Control of Detonation Processes. Moscow: ELEX KM Pub; 2000. pp. 197-209

[8] Zhdan SA, Bykovskii FA, Vedernikov FF. Mathematical modeling of a rotating detonation wave in a hydrogen-oxygen mixture. Combustion, Explosion and Shock Waves. 2007;**43**: 449-455

[9] Levin VA, Markov VV, Zhuravskaya TA, Osinkin SF. Initiation and propagation of detonation in channels of complex shape. In: Roy G, Frolov S, Shepperd J, editors. Application of Detonation to Propulsion. Moscow: TORUS PRESS Pub; 2004. pp. 71-76

[10] Taki S, Fujiwara T. A numerical study of detonation resonator. In: Roy G, Frolov S, editors. Pulse and Continuous Detonation Propulsion. Moscow: TORUS PRESS; 2006. pp. 309-320

[11] Liberman MA. Introduction to Physics and Chemistry of Combustion. Berlin-Heudelberg: Springer-Verlag; 2008

[12] Chakravarthy SR, Osher S. Lectures in Applied Mathematics. 1985;**22**(1): 57-78

[13] Semenov NN. Self deflagration and chain reactions. Uspehy Himii. 1967;**36**: 3-37

[14] Denisov ET, Sarkisov OM, Lihtenshtein GI. Chemikal Kinetic. Moscow, Russia: Himiya; 2000

[15] Saeid MH, Khadem J, Emami S, Ghodrat M. Effect of diffusion time on the mechanism of deflagration to detonation transition in an inhomogeneous mixture of hydrogen-air. International Journal of Hydrogen Energy. 2022;**47**(20):11037-11052

[16] Liu D, Liu Z, Xiao H. Flame acceleration and deflagration to detonation transition in narrow channels filled with stoichiometric hydrogen-air

mixture. International Journal of Hydrogen Energy. 2022;**47**(20): 11052-11067

[17] Martyushov SN. Numerical simulation of deflagration in hydrogen-air gas mixes. Journal of Physics: Conference Series. 2021;**2124**

[18] Toro, Eleuterio F. Riemann solvers and numerical methods for fluid dynamics: A practical introduction. 2nd ed. Berlin; Heidelberg; New York; Barcelona: Hong Kong; London; Milan; Paris; Singapore; Tokyo: Springer; 1999

[19] Ibragimova LB, Smechov GD, Shatalov OP. Recommended Rate Constants of Chemical reactions in an H2-O2 Gas Mixture withp Electronucally Excited Species O2 , O, OH Involved. Moscow: Institute of Mechanics of Moscow State University; 2003

[20] Martyushov SN, Martyushova YG. Numerical simulation of non stationary flows on the block regular grids. In: Margelov S, Vulkov L, Wasniewski J, editors. Proceedings of Fourth Conference on Numerical Analysis and Application Rousse, Bulgaria, Lectures Notes in Computer Science. Springer; 2009. p. 16

Chapter 3

Numerical Modeling Techniques to Solving Complex Geotechnical Problems: Case Studies

Qijing Yang

Abstract

This chapter will describe the numerical modeling techniques that have been used for solving the difficult geotechnical problems which cannot be solved using the conventional mechanical methods available to date due to their complexity. Two case studies will be presented in this chapter on how the problem was encountered, how the numerical modeling tool was used to appreciate the behaviors of the mechanical responses for each structural elements so that the detailed design of them can be undertaken, and how the sensitivity was done by modeling, and site instrumentation and monitoring were carried out using observational approach to validate the design predictions.

Keywords: numerical modeling, geotechnical problem, case study, bridge, tunnels

1. Introduction

The geotechnical problems encountered by a practicing engineer are often related to buildings, roads, rails, ports, tunnels, energy, and mining projects. Some of these can be evaluated with a relatively simple analytical solution, such as the bearing capacity of a pad footing with a given ground model. Others will be more complex and cannot be readily solved by simple analysis using the available theoretical equations. With the advancement of computing power and computer hardware, sophisticated three-dimensional numerical modeling techniques have gained wide applications to solving technically complex, challenging problems encountered in civil engineering. This chapter provides a brief description on how a geotechnical model can be conceptually developed, the geotechnical and hydrogeological design parameters adopted for analysis derived, design solution and the construction sequencing simulated by computer modeling. Two case studies will be presented in the following sections to demonstrate how difficult geotechnical problems can be resolved using the numerical modeling technique, which provides the basis of sound decision making.

2. Procedures for numerical modeling of geotechnical problems

The first step of the numerical modeling is to develop a conceptual ground model that will be representative of the soil, rock, and water behaviors under various boundary and loading conditions. This ground model must be established such that the controlling geological and hydrogeological features, and the construction stages closely reflect the reality. It is often an iterative process to develop such a predictive model.

Geotechnical engineering problems involving soil, rock and water are particularly complicated because natural systems exhibit spatial variability, complex and sometimes unquantifiable material behavior, and incongruent temporal and spatial scales. In many cases, physical processes are not fully understood due to limited sampling and testing data available. Consequently, an engineering judgment must be made on the results of the numerical modeling, together with validation processes during construction.

It is important to note the best numerical models should have just enough complexity for the mathematical abstraction with working hypotheses to reasonably approximate the physical reality.

It should be emphasized that the numerical modeling is a powerful tool to provide the necessary information for an engineer to make a judgment and a decision on whether the design will be acceptable or not.

3. Case study 1: piled bridge abutment

3.1 Problem description and summary

Sydney Trains commissioned Arcadis to undertake an options study and subsequent detail design for superstructure replacement of the existing steel bridge at Guess Avenue, Wolli Creek, Sydney, which was constructed around 1915. This bridge carries four tracks, with two for the Sydney main lines and two for the Illawarra lines.

One of the primary objectives was to assess if the existing timber piled abutments supporting the new bridge would be adequate or not. A site investigation was undertaken to assess the subsurface ground conditions and the quality of the existing timber piles beneath the pile cap after a desk top study of available as-built information and bridge replacement options engineering.

The case study results of both Piglet and Plaxis 3D analysis are to demonstrate how the available numerical tool enabled us to make a comprehensive assessment to utilize the existing piled foundations for the new bridge without any underpinning or foundation strengthening works [1].

3.2 New bridge concept and detail design development

There were two key issues for the new replacement bridge. One was to increase the headroom clearance from 4.13 m to 4.6 m above Guess Avenue as per current Australian code; the other was to have the new bridge designed so that it could be constructed during a period of track possession, which is usually a couple of days.

The existing steel bridge constructed around 1915 is about 27.4 m long and 20 m wide and 5.9 m high. The bridge is supported by two abutments constructed using brick works, with each resting on a group of timber piles. The pile cap is formed by

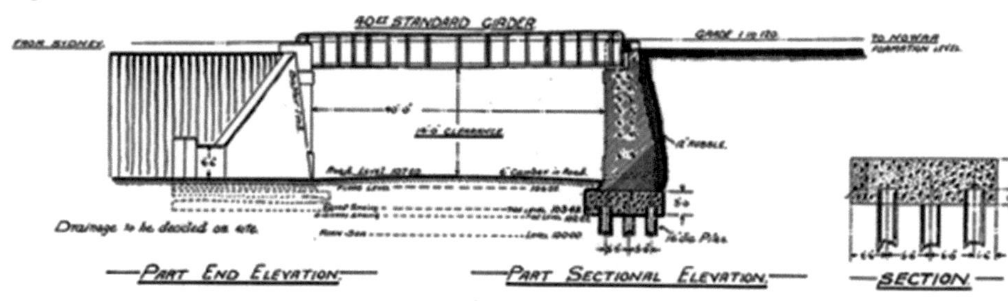

Figure 1.
Elevation of as-built bridge.

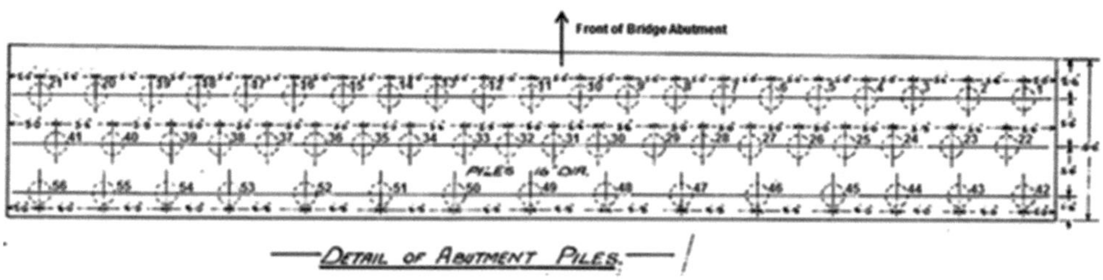

Figure 2.
Layout plan of as-built bridge abutment piles.

Loading conditions	Resultant vertical load (kN)	Resultant horizontal load (kN)	Resultant bending moment (kNm)
Existing bridge layout	9767	2969	−30
New bridge layout	12,426	1775	1156

Table 1.
SLS loading on pile foundation.

concrete, with the dimensions of 20.7 m length, 2.7 m width and 0.9 m depth. There are 56 number of 400 mm diameter timber piles in three rows based on the as-built bridge elevation and pile foundation layout plan, which are shown on **Figures 1** and **2**.

The loads acting on the top of pile foundation was provided by the bridge engineer to geotechnical engineer for pile capacity assessment. **Table 1** presents a summary of the vertical load, horizontal load and bending moment on the pile foundation under the serviceability limit state (SLS) condition. Note that the original design does not have a run-on slab between bridge abutment and the embankment, whereas the new design introduces a 3 m long run-on slab which reduces the horizontal load acting on the abutment. The bending moment was taken to be around the middle row of pile, which is the centerline of the pile cap.

3.3 Geotechnical investigations and ground model

Geotechnical investigations were carried out in two parts. The first was two cone penetration testing and the second was the excavation pits and sampling of timber piles.

Figure 3.
Exposed timber pile in an excavated pit [2].

Depth range below surface (m)	Stratum description
0.0–1.0	Concrete pavement
0.1–0.3	Cobbles/ballast
0.3–1.65	Crushed sandstone
1.65–5.5	Loose to medium dense silty sand
5.5–10.0	Medium dense to dense sand/silty sand
10–15.5	Silty sand with interbedded layers of clay/silty clay

Table 2.
Inferred subsurface profile.

The exposed timber pile during the test pit excavation, as shown in **Figure 3**, was found to be in a very good condition. The subsequent strength assessment of the cored sample indicates piles have hardly reduced in strength over 100 years.

The investigative work of two exposed piles carried out by Golder Associates [2] indicates that the measured pile diameter is only 260 mm and the center-to-center pile spacing is 860 mm, which is less than 914 mm as shown on the original layout plan and sections. The distance from the edge of the pile cap to the center of the front pile is about 430 mm, which is about 330 mm less than that shown on the original bridge drawings.

The CPT profiles show interbedded sand and clay layers of varying strength, which is typical of alluvium formation. **Table 2** shows the interpreted profile adopted for our pile foundation analysis.

3.4 Assessment of a single pile capacity

Based on the geotechnical profile presented in the above section and information contained in the geotechnical investigation report prepared by Golder Associates [2], an assessment was carried out to check if existing abutments would adequately support the new bridge superstructures.

The allowable axial structural capacity of a 260 mm diameter timber pile (Grade F22) was assessed to be 350 kN and 450 kN respectively based on a permissible axial stress of 6.6 MPa under dead load (DL) and 8.58 MPa under DL plus live load (LL). These permissible axial stresses for timber piles are based on the published guidelines by Sydney Trains (formerly Rail Corporation Infrastructure) [3].

The axial geotechnical capacity of a single timber pile was assessed using a superseded Australian Piling Code in 1978 [4]. An average ultimate shaft resistance and an ultimate end bearing resistance were assumed to be 22 kPa and 8000 kPa respectively. The ultimate geotechnical capacity of a single pile is assessed to be 550 kN based on the geological profile in **Table 2** and a pile length of 7 meters. A permissible geotechnical capacity of a single pile is derived to be 220 kN and 250 kN using a factor of safety (FOS) of 2.5 and 2.2 respectively. It was determined that for such an important bridge structure carrying four tracks, the original design would have a minimum factor of safety of 2.5. As such, a permissible geotechnical capacity of a single pile was assessed to be around 220 kN. It can be concluded from the assessment that the pile foundation design is governed by the geotechnical capacity rather than structural capacity of the timber pile.

3.5 Pile group analysis using Piglet

Two sets of pile group analyses using the commercially available program Piglet were undertaken to calculate the serviceability limit state loads on each pile. The first case assumed that the pile cap was 100% rigid and there would be no load shared by the pile cap. The other case was based on the assumptions that the pile cap would act as a raft and share 10% of vertical load. The results of the first case analyzed are presented in **Figure 4**.

The pile cap was assumed to have much greater stiffness than the timber piles beneath it such that it would be able to redistribute the loads among the piles within the group. The pile Young's modulus of the existing timber piles was assessed to be 16,000 MPa in the Piglet analysis [5], with the pile shaft shear modulus being 4000 kPa at the top increasing linearly at a gradient of 1000 kPa to the base of pile. The shear modulus of the base material immediately below the pile tip was assumed to be 50,000 kPa.

It is interesting to note that the calculated axial forces on the front row of piles, as shown on **Figure 4**, are around 250 kN, with up to 500 kN on the edge piles, which is likely to exceed the permissible pile capacity of 220 kN. The load on the middle row is generally around 150 kN whereas the load on the back row is close to 220 kN. When the pile cap shares 10% of the vertical load, there is an opportunity to bring the axial load on the front row of piles down close to the assessed permissible pile capacity of 220 kN, except for the edge piles. The loads on the remaining piles are less than the permissible capacity of 220 kN. These results provided us with a level of confidence to propose to Sydney Trains that underpinning or strengthening for the pile foundations may not be required when piled raft concept is appropriately considered for the load redistribution among piles.

3.6 Plaxis 3D analysis and results

Plaxis 3D model simulated for a single abutment only based on the similar nature of both abutments and the limitation of size of mesh and calculation time. The timber piles were simulated as structural element and brick abutment was modeled as physical material "blocks". The approach slab was modeled as structural elements.

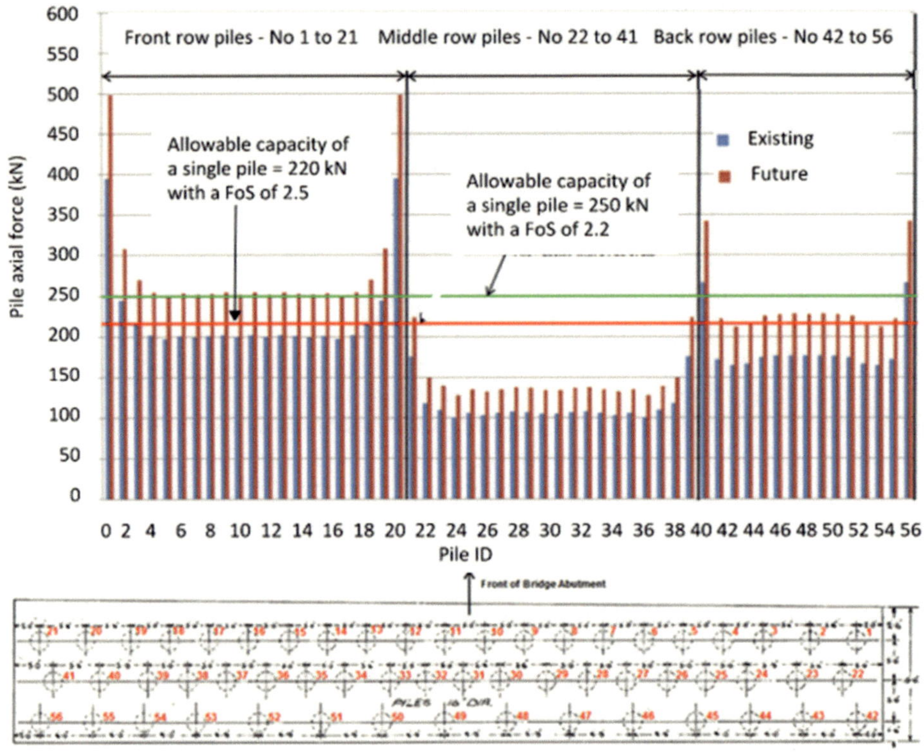

Figure 4.
Calculated pile loads for existing and new bridge by Piglet.

Typical printout of the generated mesh and the applied loads are presented in **Figure 5**. The dead load and live load of the existing bridge was modeled as point loads, whereas the new bridge loads were simulated as uniformly distributed loads, as shown on **Figure 5**. Based on AS5100 [6], the train loads resulting from four tracks were modeled as four equivalent uniformly distributed loads (UDL) of 80 kPa, with the first and second tracks being at 100 percent and the remaining are 85% and 70% of UDL at the third and fourth tracks respectively.

The load application sequences of Plaxis 3D modeling are described as follows:

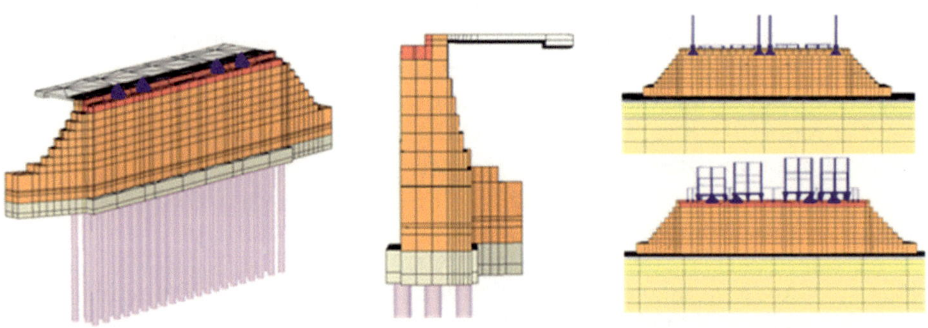

Figure 5.
Plaxis 3D model in different perspective view.

Case ID	Case description
Case 1	Existing bridge load plus train loading (100%/100%/85%/70% UDL)
Case 2	Existing bridge load plus train loading (70%/85%/100%/100% UDL)
Case 1A	New bridge 320 kN/m line load f plus train loading (100%/100%/85%/70% UDL)
Case 2A	New bridge 320 kN/m line load plus train loading (70%/85%/100%/100% UDL)
Case1A1	New bridge 350 kN/m line load plus train loading (100%/100%/100%/100% UDL)
Case2A2	New bridge 350 kN/m line load plus train loading (100%/100%/100%/100% UDL)

Table 3.
A summary of Plaxis 3D cases analyzed.

- Dead load of the proposed bridge superstructure on each abutment
- Live load of the proposed bridge superstructure
- Approach slab dead load onto the back of headstock
- Approach slab live load onto the back of headstock
- Remaining dead load of approach slab
- Remaining live load on approach slab
- Rail surcharge

A total of six Plaxis 3D cases were analyzed. A summary of each case ID and its associated loading description is presented in **Table 3**.

It is noted that the sequencing of the train track loading is not sensitive to the maximum calculated axial force on the pile foundation. It can be seen from **Figure 6** that the maximum axial load for on pile is around 250 kN for both existing and new bridge loads, with the majority of piles well below 200 kN. Further sensitive analyses with 100% UDL on all tracks yields similar maximum axial force on piles. This implies that the pile group capacity is adequate to carry the additional loads from the proposed new bridge superstructure when the pile cap contribution is appropriately considered.

Sensitivity analyses for the new bridge loads were carried out for a higher line load of 350 kN/m, which is approximately 10% higher than 320 kN/m, and 100% UDL train load for all tracks. The calculated pile axial load increases, as shown on **Figure 7**, are less than 5% as compared to those for the standard load cases. This suggests the pile group system would not be overstressed due to potentially increased train loads except for a few piles among the 56 piles.

A high level of confidence was built upon the results of Plaxis 3D modeling for various loading conditions described in **Table 3**. Arcadis was subsequently able to recommend that the existing timber piled foundations and brick abutments be used for new bridge replacement works without any underpinning or strengthening.

3.7 Construction of the new replacement bridge

Two separate superstructures were installed during two (2) consecutive weekend track possessions of approximately 48 hours each. The first one was at the end of June 2015 and the other at the beginning of July 2015. Prior to the first track

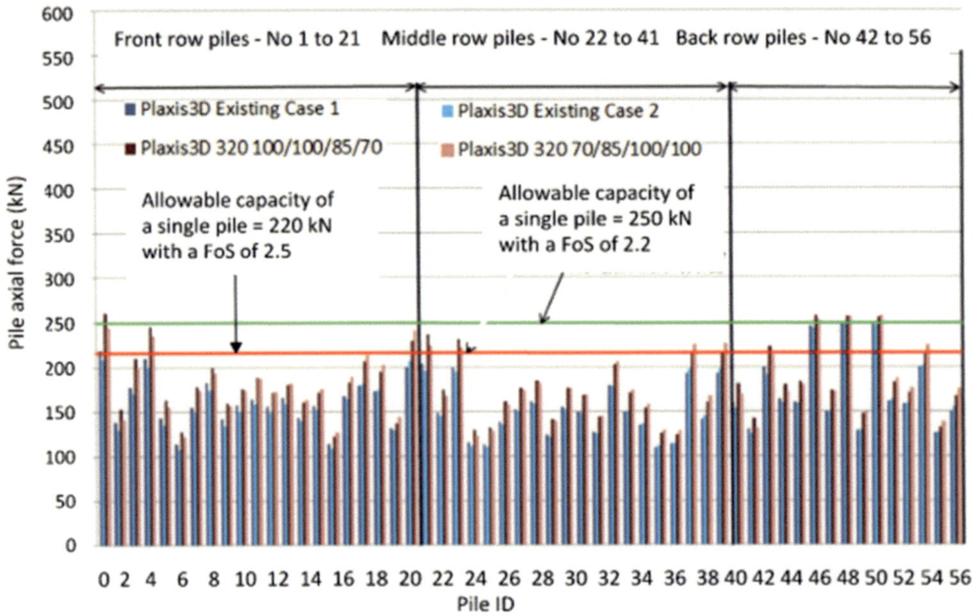

Figure 6.
Calculated axial forces for existing and new bridge loads using Plaxis 3D.

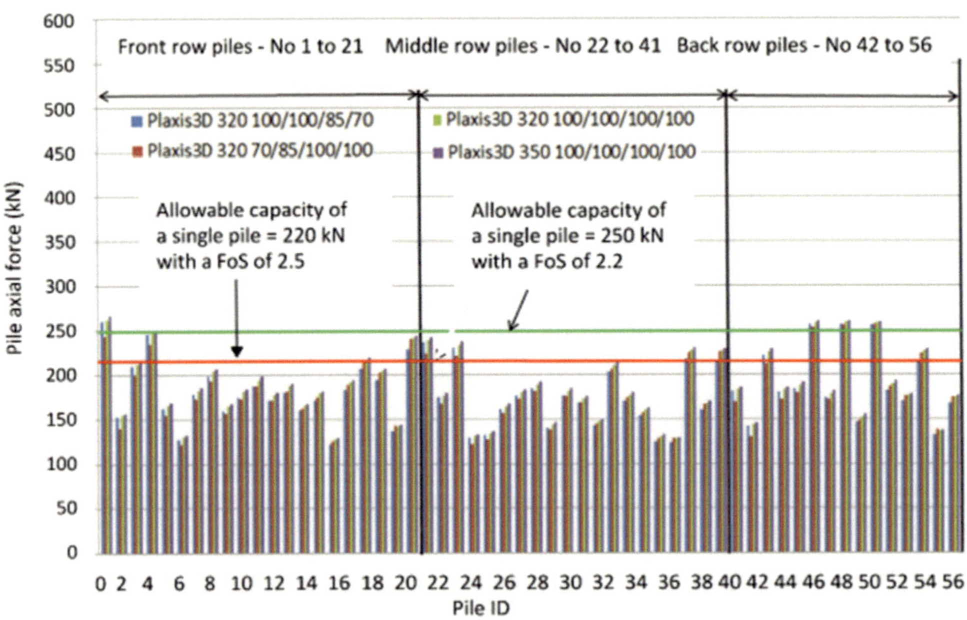

Figure 7.
Calculated axial forces for different new bridge loads using Plaxis 3D.

possession, a 750 tonne crawler crane was assembled adjacent to the Sydney side abutment, beside the railway tracks.

Horizontal saw cutting of the abutment ledges to accommodate the proposed precast concrete headstocks was carried out on the Friday afternoon of each track

Figure 8.
Constructed new replacement bridge.

possession. Temporary steel stitching plates were installed across the cut lines to prevent any differential movement/separation due to the action of rail traffic in the period leading up to the actual possession.

Figure 8 shows the constructed bridge superstructure, with all four train tracks. The movement observed during, and post construction was found to be less than originally predicted.

3.8 Conclusions

The upgrading of Guess Avenue underbridge with filler beam deck unit superstructures represented an appropriate solution for this project site, which satisfied Sydney Trains' project objectives. These were primarily to increase the vertical clearance to the road below, re-use the existing substructures and to construct a bridge upgrading form of construction that represents reduced maintenance.

This case study demonstrated that the importance of soil and structure interaction in the pile group analysis, and the contribution of plie cap to the pile group capacity. It is also found that Piglet analysis would overestimate the maximum axial pile force at the edge of pile group. Plaxis 3D modeling shows that the load distribution among the front row of piles is relatively uniform without any spike for the edge piles. Further sensitivity analyses using Plaxis 3D indicate that the pile group has adequate capacity when the piled-raft concept is appropriately considered. This enabled Arcadis to recommend Sydney Trains to construct the new replacement bridge superstructure without any underpinning or strengthening works for the timber piled foundations and brick abutments.

The limited monitoring results indicate that the abutment movements during and post bridge superstructure construction are within the original prediction.

4. Case study 2: Sydney Metro Martin place south shaft excavation impact assessment

4.1 Project description and summary

Sydney Metro City & Southwest Tunnel Station Excavation (TSE) section is twin 15.5 km tunnels between Chatswood and Sydenham Station, with the tunneling beneath Sydney Harbor and CBD constructed using five tunnel boring machines (TBMs). It includes excavation of six new underground metro stations at Crows Nest, Victoria Cross, Barangaroo, Martin Place, Pitt Street and Waterloo. The TSE contract was awarded John Holland, CPB Contractors and Ghella Joint Venture (JHCBPG) in 2018, which was Australia's biggest public transport project at the time.

The primary design team included Arcadis, BG&E, PSM and NOMA Consulting. Herein presents the impact assessment of the Martin Place south shaft (MPSS) excavation and future development of Macquarie Bank Building on the existing Eastern Suburban Railway (ESR) tunnel lining structure. METRON, which is an advisory body to Sydney Metro, was formed by Matt MacDonald and Arcadis as well as Sydney Metro staff who were responsible for planning and approval of the Sydney Metro design and construction.

The layout plan, as shown in **Figure 9** [7], includes Martin Place south shafts (northern and southern sections) adits (A4, A4d, A5a, A5b, A7 and A8), new metro station cavern and running tunnels together with the existing ESR tunnels. The proposed excavations for the proposed station works will reduce the rock pillars as slender as 3.1 m, rock cover above the ESR crown just 2.6 m, and a minimum rock beam thickness below the ESR invert of only 2.3 m at localized places.

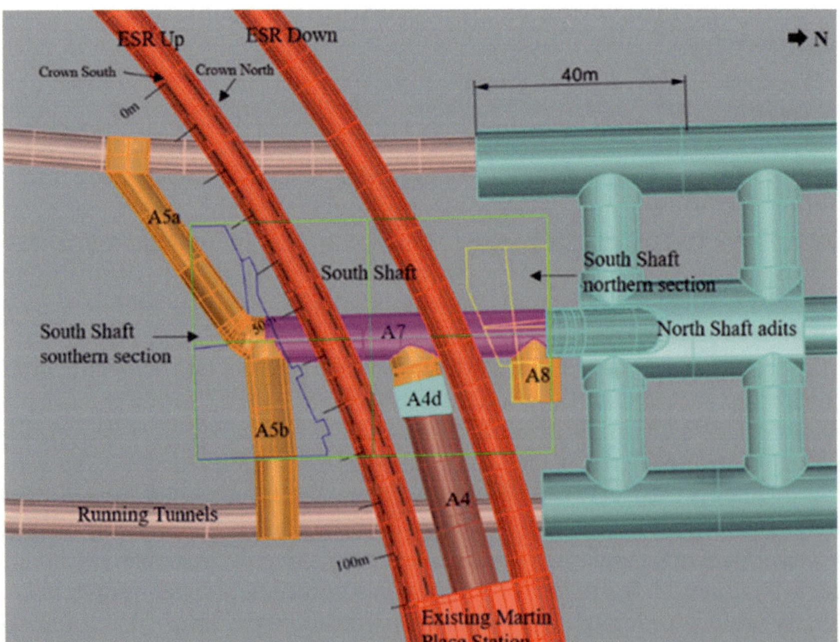

Figure 9.
Martin Place Station excavations and existing ESR tunnels [7].

The potential impacts of the proposed excavations and long-term building loading on the existing ESR tunnels were carried out by JHCPBG (temporary shaft excavation) using both 2D and 3D analysis software packages. METRON was requested to undertake an independent assessment to ensure the final decision can be made if the JHCPBG proposed excavation and the support system is adequate.

In this independent assessment, both 2D and 3D numerical modeling was carried out to confirm the following:

The possible lower and upper bound of the predicted vertical and horizonal displacements of the up and down track linings of ESR tunnels. Sensitivity analysis was also used to evaluate the key parameters that would cause significant impacts. The excavation and support process and mitigation measures that enabled JHCPBG to implement, based on the monitored displacement of the tunnel lining. As such, the design by JHCPBG was accepted using the observational approach with instrumentation and live monitoring of ESR tunnels, plus grouting and mesh protective works of tunnel roofs after extensive numerical modeling works. This case study will show the utility of numerical modeling tools for analysing complex underground excavation problem and highlight the importance of engineering judgment in decision making.

4.2 Site investigations and model development

Site investigations at Martin Place Station included the borehole drilling of soils and coring of rock plus RAAX imaging. The geological mapping information of the adjacent basement excavations and the existing ESR tunnel mapping data was made available. A summary of the subsurface profile at the proposed Martin Place Station is presented in **Table 4**. It can be noted that the majority of the south shaft excavation will be through class I/II sandstone. The key geological features identified were the presence of high in-situ stress in Hawkesbury sandstone, the Martin Place Joint Swarm and other geological features in parallel to the GPO Fault Zone in the vicinity of the proposed shaft excavation.

A typical geological section through Adit 7 considered in the design, as shown in **Figure 10**, is to capture the greatest change to ESR tunnel lining stress and strain conditions.

The numerical models considered include a design base case, an adverse case, and sensitivity cases to cover the possible scenarios. Not all mapped information of the existing ESR tunnels were not modeled precisely because the generation of such a

Unit	Reduced level of top of unit (m, AHD)		Thick-ness (m)	Description
	West	East		
Fill	18.5–22.5	22.4–27	0–2	Variable
Hawkesbury sand-stone	17–19.5	22–25.5	>50	Class IV and V with variable thickness (up to 3–5 m), absent at some places and overlying class III. Class I/II sandstone is generally encountered at depth. However deeper zones of class III and IV are also expected at depth in association with the geological features of Marin Place Joint Swarm and GPO Fault Zone

Table 4.
Inferred sub-surface conditions at Martin Place Station [8].

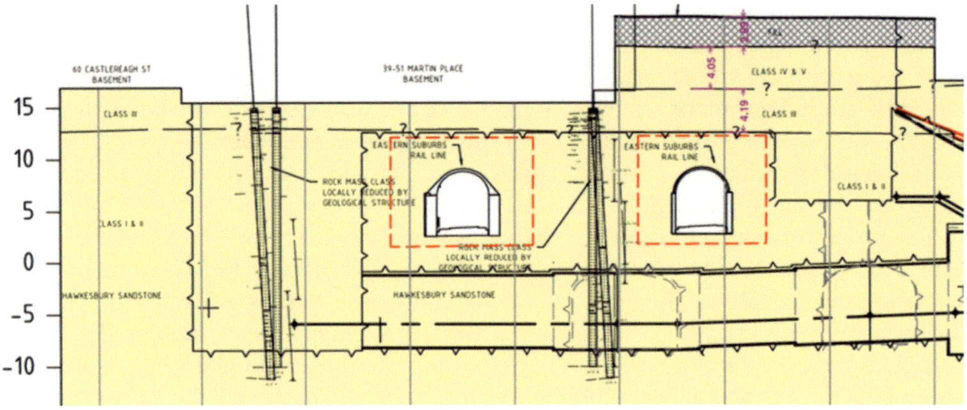

Figure 10.
Ground profile adopted in PLAXIS 3D analysis [8].

complex 3D model would require significantly more time, funding and computing power except for key geological features.

4.3 Model parameters

Material parameters for modeling the rock mass were adopted from the south shaft Geotechnical Design Report [8] (for rock mass properties). For models of the jointed rock mass the parameters derived for the JHCPBG UDEC (intact rock properties, joint strength/stiffness and joint distribution, alignment and standard deviation) were adopted [8].

Both elastic and elastic plastic tunnel lining parameters were considered in modeling. Where the lining was modeled as an elastic/plastic material, a Tresca failure criterion was adopted with a UCS of 21 MPa and a tensile cut-off of 1.8 MPa.

Interfaces between the lining and rock mass and at "cold joints" were also allowed for within the modeling. Properties for these interfaces were as per the TSE modeling [8].

In situ stresses have been adopted from the JHCPBG modeling [8] and two in-situ stress conditions, as shown in **Table 5**, were considered for the 2D models:

- Major horizontal principal stress acting in plane for sensitivity study only
- Minor horizontal principal stress acting in plane as per UDEC model—ref to [8]

Rock class	Low stress*	Field stress*
Sandstone IV/V	$\sigma_H = \sigma_h = \sigma_v$	$\sigma_H = \sigma_h = \sigma_v$
Sandstone III	$\sigma_H = \sigma_h = \sigma_v$	$\sigma_H = \sigma_{NS} = 2.0\sigma_v$ $\sigma_h = \sigma_{EW} = 0.6\sigma_H$
Sandstone I/II	$\sigma_H = \sigma_h = \sigma_v$	$\sigma_H = \sigma_{NS} = 2.0\sigma_v + 2.5$ MPa $\sigma_h = \sigma_{EW} = 0.7\sigma_H$

**where σ_v is the vertical stress; σ_H is the major principal horizontal stress; σ_h is the minor principal horizontal stress; σ_{NS} is the principal horizontal stress in the north-south direction; and σ_{EW} is the principal horizontal stress in the east-west direction.*

Table 5.
In situ stresses of various rock classes considered in the modeling.

Sandstone class	I	II	II	IV
Density (kN/m^3)	24	24	24	24
UCS (MPa)	30	25	15	10
Cohesion (kPa)	1000	500	300	200
Friction angle (deg)	55	50	50	40
Tensile strength (kPa)	<300	<100	<20	<10
Mass Young's Modulus (MPa)	3000	2000	1000	500

Table 6.
Rock mass parameters adopted for Plaxis 3D analysis.

The rock mass properties adopted for Plaxis 3D analysis, based on Mohr Coulomb failure criteria, is summarized in **Table 6**.

4.4 Modeling approach and construction staging

For the METRON comparative exercise program RS2 was used. RS2 models a jointed rock mass as a continuum with the inclusion of joints. Elastoplastic deformation can be modeled along these joints, but the blocks are not free to move and interact for large strain problems as per UDEC by JHCPBG. For small strain problems the joints in UDEC remain relatively tight and independent block movement will be retained. The solutions at small strain will therefore be comparable to the RS2 continuum. The sequencing modeled in RS2 is as follows:

1. Tunnel lining installed;
2. Excavate To 12.5 m—uniform excavation above tunnels to RL 12.5 m;
3. Excavate North shaft—excavate north shaft to RL 6.0 m;
4. Excavate Adit 4—Adit 4 excavated and fully relaxed without support;
5. Exc. South shaft—south shaft excavated to –RL 6.5 m; and
6. Loading increase to a total of 100 kPa—100 kPa applied over area between tunnels with remainder being 20 kPa.

The modeled excavation and support sequencing adopted in Plaxis 3D to compare the result against FLAC 3D by JHCPBG are as follows:

1. Initial in-situ stress conditions;
2. Excavation of the existing ESR tunnels;
3. Existing basements for the adjacent buildings;
4. Excavate southern entrance shaft to RL 12.5 m (all displacements will be re-set to zero at the start of this stage);

5. Excavate mini shaft to the final design level;

6. Excavate and construct mini shaft (A4s) to Adit A4;

7. Excavate southern entrance shaft north side to final excavation level;

8. Excavate and construct Adit A7;

9. Excavate and construction Adit A4a, A4b and A4c the connections between the Adits A4 and A7;

10. Excavate southern entrance shaft south side to the final excavation level; and

11. Changing the surcharge loading at RL 12.5 to 100 kPa as per the design for future development requirements.

4.5 Results of 2D independent numerical modeling

Figure 11 shows the mesh generated by RS2 in the vicinity of the existing ESR tunnels, the proposed south shafts (northern and southern sections). The calculated displacements at various points of the tunnels by RS2 are also presented in **Figure 12**. The following observations could be made from three different types of RS2 model analyses:

- The RS2 model is comparative to the JHCPBG UDEC model
- Continuum models tend to overpredict lining displacements
- Within jointed models, lining displacement magnitudes are heavily influenced by the explicit joint pattern

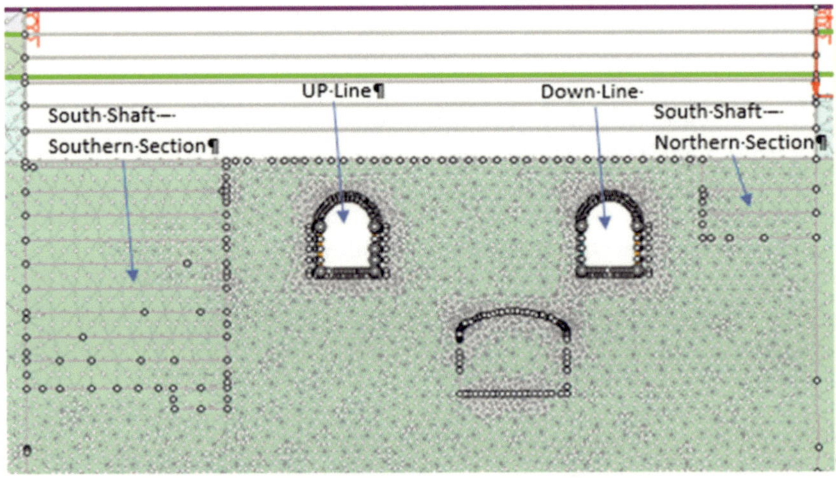

Figure 11.
Mesh from RS2 showing ESR up and down tunnels, south shafts and Adit 4.

Figures 13 and **14** indicate the magnitude of variance of the calculated displacements at nominated points surrounding the down line and up line tunnels for the jointed model. It can also be noted from these figures that the JHCPBG results

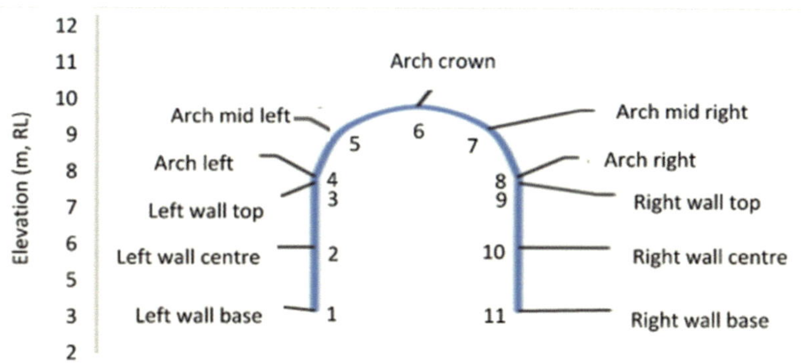

Figure 12.
Point ID for reporting calculated displacements around ESR tunnel.

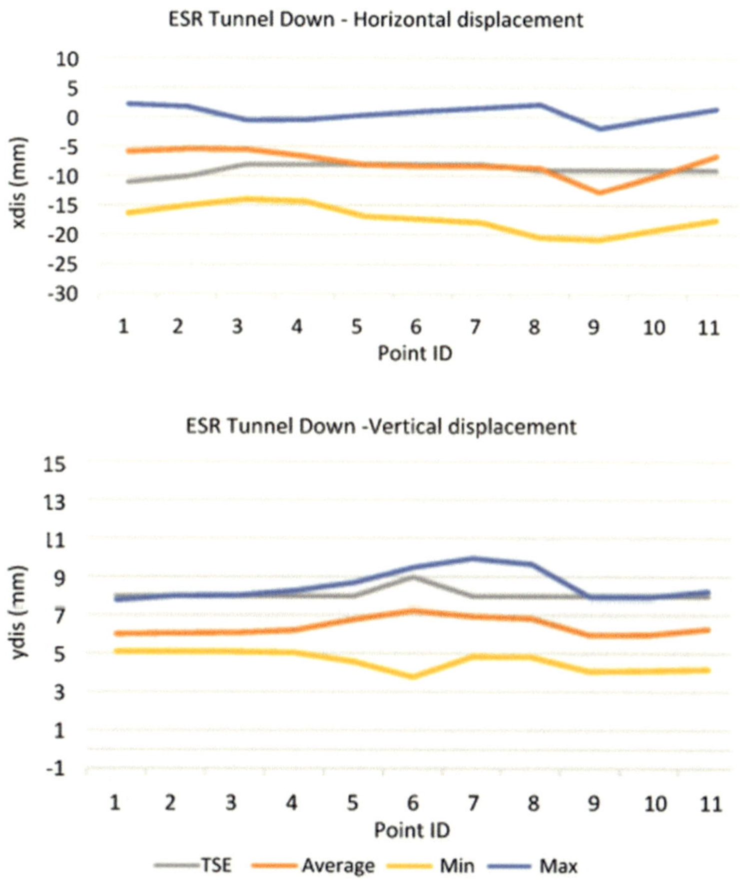

Figure 13.
Maximum, minimum and average horizontal and vertical displacements of lining intrados of down line compared to JHCPBG results at end of excavation stage.

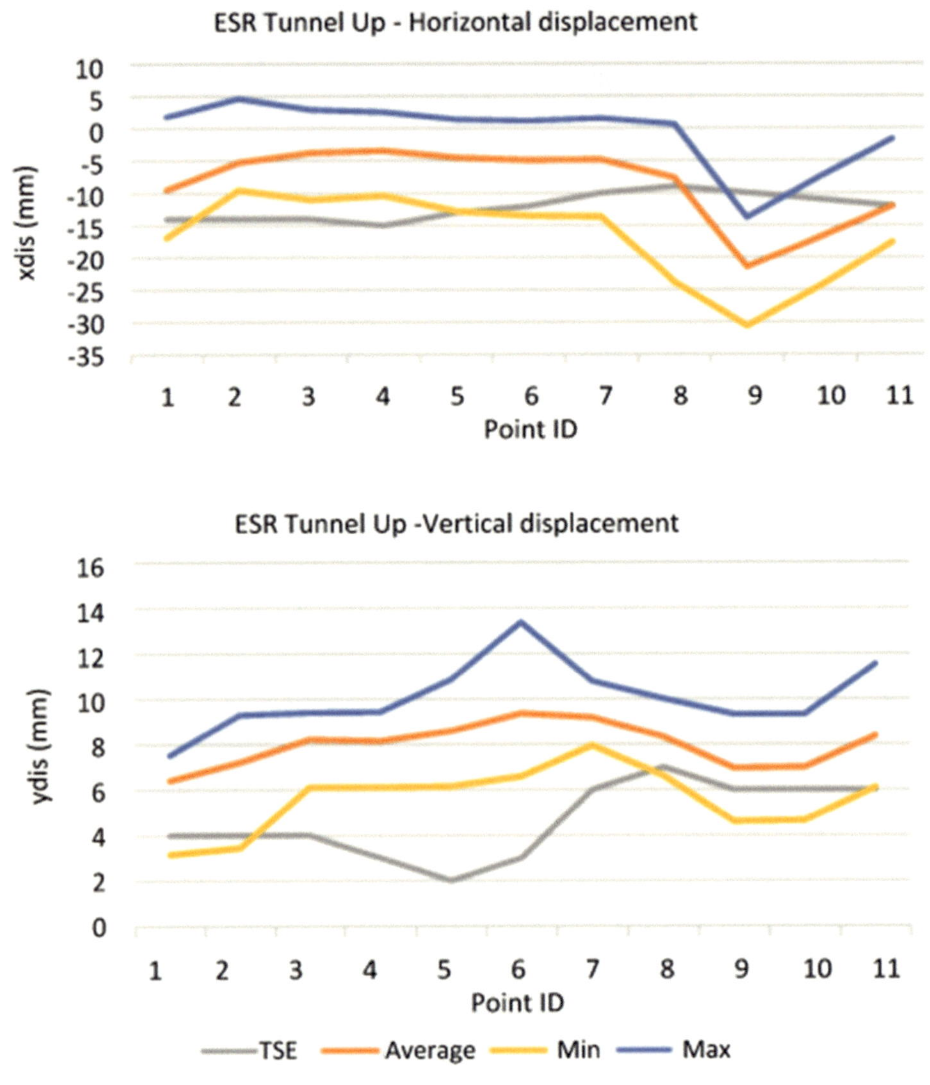

Figure 14.
Maximum, minimum and average horizontal and vertical displacement of lining intrados of up line compared to JHCPBG results at end of excavation stage.

generally lie within the range of the RS2 results, with the average case being in good agreement with the design case, and maximum with the adverse case.

4.6 Results of 3D independent numerical modeling

Plaxis 3D modeling, as shown in **Figure 15**, was undertaken based on the given geometry and geotechnical design parameters adopted by JHCPBG design. The construction sequencing was the same as those described in Section 4.4.

The modeling results indicate that the maximum lateral displacement in ESR tunnel is approximately 12 mm for the design base case with about 20 mm for the adverse case due to south shaft excavation, as shown in **Figure 16**. These are slightly lower than values of 16 mm and 25 mm by JHCPBG respectively.

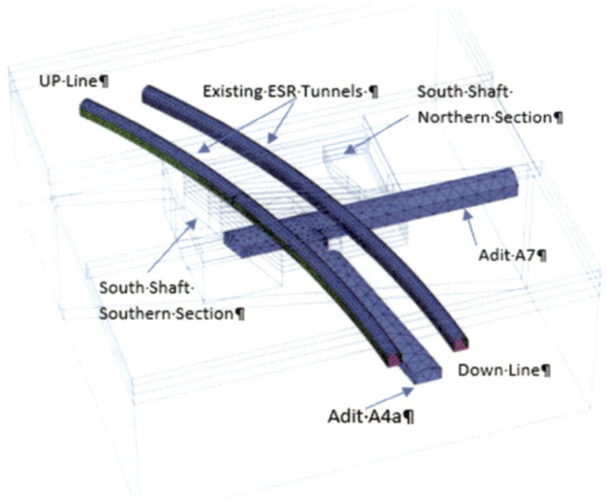

Figure 15.
Plaxis 3D model show the south shaft excavation and ESR tunnels.

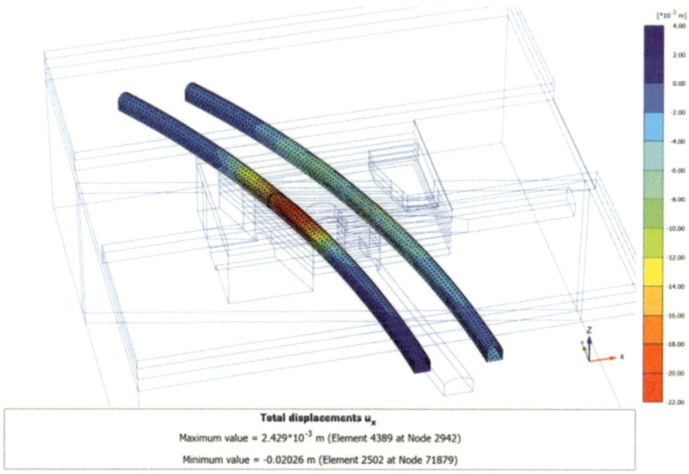

Figure 16.
Horizontal displacement (Ux) for the existing ESR tunnels at the end of excavation as per JHCPBG design—stage 10.

The additional load of the proposed mini shaft A4S will result in about 2–3 mm displacement. The future development loading of 80 kPa will cause less than 1 mm movement at the ESR tunnel lining.

4.7 Modeling observations and discussions

The 2D and 3D modeling results and comparison study indicates the following:

- The jointed RS2 model replicates the results of the JHCPBG UDEC model reasonably well as this modeling approach is similar to that of UDEC when any unstable blocks will be mapped and stabilized in a staged and controlled manner.

- The increased displacements and loads within the lining, due to future loading of 80 kPa equivalent UDL, are small compared to the displacements and loads imposed by the proposed excavation.

- Lining displacements within the RS2 model are highly sensitive to the adopted joint pattern as expected.

- Plaxis 3D analysis shows that the effect of the mini shaft excavation on the existing ESR tunnel are not significant, and the additional displacement caused by the mini shaft excavation is approximately 2–3 mm.

- PLAXIS 3D model shows that the 2D analysis results are likely to overestimate lining displacements and that "out of plane" geometry has the potential to significantly reduce displacements due to the buttressing effects.

Discussions with Sydney Metro staff were held to fully appreciate the likely range of predicted displacements of ESR tunnel lining induced by south shaft excavation, with the following two important fundamental facts:

- The displacements due to high in-situ stresses within the rock mass immediate surrounding the ESR tunnels would have been partly released during construction stage, hence the predicted movements of the ESR tunnel lining are likely to be overestimated.

- The stiffness of the clay filled materials occurred at varying depths would not sustain high in-situ stresses, for example, where joint swarms are present. Consequently, the predicted lateral displacements of the ESR tunnel lining would be on the high side.

Based on the above the independent modeling results, it was recommended that JHCPBG design be accepted by Sydney Metro.

4.8 Instrumentation and monitoring

Live monitoring of the excavation and ESRL were proposed during the excavation (as advised by JHCPBG) to confirm the results of the numerical analyses. The monitoring points are set out in either 2 m center to center at the critical locations, or 4 m center to center along the tunnel alignment. A typical instrumentation layout points for the ESR tunnel lining is shown in **Figure 17** [7].

Hold points were stipulated during the excavation phase to allow JHCPBG and Sydney Metro to review any additional data (mapping and monitoring), review model performance considering this additional information, calibrate models if deemed to be necessary and allow excavation/loading to take place. Key stages of the excavation were at:

- Excavation to RL 12.5 m

- Excavation of northern part of southern access shaft to RL 6.0 m

- Excavation of Adit 4

- Excavation of southern section of southern access shaft to RL −6.3 m

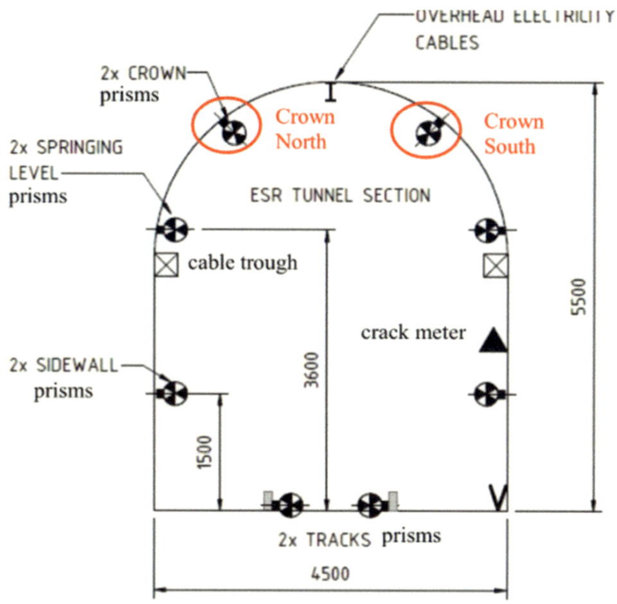

Figure 17.
Proposed ESR tunnel instrument layout (after 7).

A dilapidation survey of the existing ESR tunnels was carried out, including coring and assessment of the lining, and as a consequence, installation of protective mesh in the crown of the existing tunnels. Details are beyond the scope of this book chapter.

4.9 Construction control and site validation

Review comments from METRON were incorporated in the AFC design drawings including the appropriate implementation of the observational approach to the following:

- Instrumentation and live monitoring points for the ESR tunnels and hold points as well as the action plans associated with the trigger values documented on the Drawing shall be implemented.

- Any available monitoring data is made available for review and compared to the results of JHCPBG's modeling to verify assumptions and model performance, prior to progression of the excavation and subsequent loading.

- Any available excavation mapping data is made available for review and compared to JHCPBG's modeling assumptions prior to progression of the excavation and subsequent loading above the ESR tunnel lining.

- Further calibration of the modeling may be required considering any additional information received.

The monitored horizontal and vertical displacements range from less than 1 mm up to 3–5 mm. The Up tunnel crown recorded a maximum lateral displacement of

5 mm and 5 mm vertical displacement the down tunnel recorded 4 mm laterally and 5 mm vertically [7], which are less than predicted.

5. Conclusions

This case study indicates that the use of numerical modeling tools to provide useful class A predictions for the base case solution together with lower and upper sensitivity results. The measured movements were less than predicted and live train operation were running successfully without any disruption during the shaft excavations.

Acknowledgements

The author would like to thank Sydney Trains for providing this project opportunity of working on this challenging project - Case 1. Ken Maxwell, who is the project manager and bridge engineer, is greatly appreciated for his support and contribution to the success of this project. The author is indebted to the geotechnical team who carried out Plaxis 3D modeling works for this project.

The success of the project - Case 2 was indebted to guidance from Sydney Metro and Transport for NSW during planning and implementation. John Holland, CPB Ghella JV for design and construction innovations, the cooperation among consultants Arcadis BG&E, PSM, NOMA Consulting, Mott MacDonald are also greatly appreciated, Special thanks are due to Dr. Owen Davis and Dr. Bo Xu for their analysis and review works and Mike Baron for his management of the works presented in the second case study on Martin Place Station works.

Author details

Qijing Yang
Arcadis Australia Pacific Pty Ltd, Sydney, Australia

*Address all correspondence to: jim.yang@arcadis.com

References

[1] Yang QJ. A case study of numerical modelling solution to practical piled bridge foundation problems. In: Proc. 15th International Conference of the International Association of Computer Methods and Advances in Geomechanics. Wuhan, China: Organising Committee of the Conference; Oct. 19-23, 2017

[2] Golder Associates: Geotechnical Investigation of Existing Foundations, Hyder-Guess Avenue Railway Underbridge, Wolli Creek, Report No. Sydney, Australia: Golder Associates as it is a Company; 117622019_003_R_Rev0. 2012

[3] Rail Infrastructure Corporation: Methodology for Load Rating of Timer Underbridge, Infrastructure Engineering Manual, C2222, Version 1.0, Sydney, Australia: Rail Infrastructure Corporation; 2001

[4] Australian Standard: ASS Piling Code: Piling Code, AS2159-1978. North Sydney, Australia: Standards Association of Australia; 1978

[5] Australian Standard: Timber Structure, Part-1: Design Method, AS1720.1-2010. Sydney, Australia: SAI Global Limited under licence from Standards Australia Limited; 2010

[6] Australian Standard: Bridge Design, AS5100-2004. Sydney, Australia: Standards Australia International Limited; 2004

[7] Packer M, He K, Rouvray B, de Ambrosis A. Sydney Metro Martin Place Station South Shaft – back-analysis case study of ground displacements adjacent to existing railway tunnels. In: Proceedings of the 14th Australia and New Zealand Conference on Geomechanics. Cairns, Australia: Organising Committee of Conference; 2023 (ANZ2023)

[8] Holland J. CPB Contractors & Ghella, AFC Report on Sydney Metro City & Southwest – TSE, Design Package: DP-T-131, SM MUSP Martin Place Station SOUTH Cavern & Adit - Excavation & Primary Support. Report No: CSWTSE-JNM-SMP-CX-RPT-830002. Sydney, Australia: Holland, CPB Contractor & Ghella as it is a Company for the Design and Construction Contract; 2019

Chapter 4

On the 1-Parameter Trigonometric and Hyperbolic Inequalities Chains

Abd Raouf Chouikha

Abstract

In this chapter, we introduce other classes of inequalities chains depending on a parameter, extending the classical ones. We show in particular how the Huygens and Wilker inequalities are related in chains. We thus improve the recent results of Chen and Mortici.

Keywords: trigonometric functions, Analytic inequalities, Sinc functions, Wilker inequality, Cusa inequality

1. Introduction

Wilker [1] presented the following inequality of great importance since it inspired many researchers (see [2–7] and references therein), for $x \in \left(0, \frac{\pi}{2}\right)$,

$$\left(\frac{\sin x}{x}\right)^2 + \frac{\tan x}{x} > 2. \tag{1}$$

Furthermore, we have equivalence between inequalities

$$\cos x < \left(\frac{\sin x}{x}\right)^3 \Leftrightarrow 1 < \left(\frac{\sin x}{x}\right)^2 \frac{\tan x}{x}, \qquad 0 < x < \frac{\pi}{2}.$$

By using the arithmetic-geometric mean inequality, Baricz and Sandor [8] have pointed out that this inequality implies

$$\frac{2\sin x}{x} + \frac{\tan x}{x} > 3 \quad and \quad \left(\frac{\sin x}{x}\right)^2 + \frac{\tan x}{x} > 2$$

The following inequality is due to Huygens for $0 < x < \frac{\pi}{2}$

$$\frac{\sin x}{x} + \frac{\tan x}{2x} > \frac{3}{2}. \tag{2}$$

The following inequality valid for $x \in \left(0, \frac{\pi}{2}\right)$, is known as Cusa inequality

$$\frac{\sin x}{x} < \frac{2}{3} + \frac{\cos x}{3}.$$

Inspired by Wilker inequality, Wu and Srivastava [9] have introduced a similar inequality of Wilker type:

$$\left(\frac{x}{\sin x}\right)^2 + \frac{x}{\tan x} > 2. \tag{3}$$

These inequalities were widely extended to cases related to Bessel functions [2], Lemniscate functions [3], mixed trigonometric-polynomial problems [10–12], asymptotic expansions [1, 6, 9], generalized hyperbolic functions.

In Ref. [2] the authors compared these two inequalities as well as the similar inequalities and provided for $x \in \left(0, \frac{\pi}{2}\right)$,

$$\frac{\sin x}{x} + \frac{\tan x}{2x} + \frac{1}{2} < \left(\frac{\sin x}{x}\right)^2 + \frac{\tan x}{x}. \tag{4}$$

$$\frac{x}{\sin x} + \frac{x}{2\tan x} + \frac{1}{2} < \left(\frac{x}{\sin x}\right)^2 + \frac{x}{\tan x}. \tag{5}$$

Analog results occur for the hyperbolic functions.

More precisely, the authors proved the following chain ([13], Theorem 2.1 or Theorem 4.1) for $x \in \left(0, \frac{\pi}{2}\right)$,

$$\frac{1}{2}\left[\left(\frac{\sin x}{x}\right)^2 + \frac{\tan x}{x}\right] > \frac{1}{3}\left[\frac{2\sin x}{x} + \frac{\tan x}{x}\right] >$$

$$\frac{1}{2}\left[\left(\frac{x}{\sin x}\right)^2 + \frac{x}{\tan x}\right] > \frac{1}{3}\left[\frac{2x}{\sin x} + \frac{x}{\tan x}\right] > 1. \tag{6}$$

For the hyperbolic counterpart, they proved the analog chain ([13], Theorem 2.2 or Theorem 4.2) for $x \in (0, \infty)$,

$$\frac{1}{2}\left[\left(\frac{\sinh x}{x}\right)^2 + \frac{\tanh x}{x}\right] > \frac{1}{3}\left[\frac{2\sinh x}{x} + \frac{\tanh x}{x}\right] >$$

$$\frac{1}{2}\left[\left(\frac{x}{\sinh x}\right)^2 + \frac{x}{\tanh x}\right] > \frac{1}{3}\left[\frac{2x}{\sinh x} + \frac{x}{\tanh x}\right] > 1. \tag{7}$$

The following inequality which is the hyperbolic counterpart is due to Lazarevic, for $x \neq 0$

$$\left(\frac{\sinh x}{x}\right)^3 > \cosh x.$$

Moreover, in [4] Chen and Mortici showed how the Huygens and Wilker inequalities are related. In this sense, they established a class of inequalities depending on a parameter n, where Huygens and Wilker inequalities are obtained when n = 1 and n = 2, respectively.

More precisely they proved the following results.

Theorems 1, 2, 3 For every integer $n > 1$ and $0 < x < \left(0, \frac{\pi}{2}\right)$, we have

$$\left(\frac{\sin x}{x}\right)^n + \frac{n \tan x}{2x} - \frac{n+2}{x} > 0, \tag{8}$$

$$\left(\frac{x}{\sin x}\right)^n + \frac{nx}{2 \tan x} - \frac{n+2}{2} > 0. \tag{9}$$

For every integer $n \geq 2$ and $0 < x < \left(0, \frac{\pi}{2}\right)$, we have

$$\left(\frac{\sin x}{x}\right)^n - \frac{n}{3} \cos x + \frac{n-3}{3} > 0. \tag{10}$$

In fact, we provide the following chains depending in n which improves Theorem 1 of [4] and inequality (4) of [2].

Theorem A *For every integer* $n \geq 1$ *and* $x \in \left(0, \frac{\pi}{2}\right)$, *we have*

$$\begin{aligned} 0 &< \frac{\sin x}{x} + \frac{\tan x}{2x} - \frac{3}{2} < \left(\frac{\sin x}{x}\right)^2 + \frac{\tan x}{x} - 2 < \dots \\ &< f(n,x) = \left(\frac{\sin x}{x}\right)^n + \frac{n \tan x}{2x} - \frac{n+x}{x}. \end{aligned} \tag{11}$$

This inequality becomes Huygens and Wilker inequality for n = 1 and n = 2, respectively.

Theorem B *For every integer* $n \geq 1$ *and* $x \in \left(0, \frac{\pi}{2}\right)$, *we have*

$$\begin{aligned} 0 &< \frac{x}{\sin x} + \frac{x}{2 \tan x} - \frac{3}{2} < \left(\frac{x}{\sin x}\right)^2 + \frac{x}{\tan x} - 2 < \dots \\ &< g(n,x) = \left(\frac{x}{\sin x}\right)^n + \frac{nx}{2 \tan x} - \frac{n+2}{2}. \end{aligned} \tag{12}$$

Theorem B improves Theorem 2 of [4] and inequality (5) of [2].

Theorem C *For every integer* $n \geq 2$ *and* $x \in \left(0, \frac{\pi}{2}\right)$, *we have*

$$\begin{aligned} 0 &< \left(\frac{\sin x}{x}\right)^2 - \frac{2 \cos x}{3} - \frac{1}{3} < \left(\frac{\sin x}{x}\right)^3 - \cos x < \cdots \\ &< \left(\frac{\sin x}{x}\right)^n - \frac{n \cos x}{3} + \frac{n-3}{3}. \end{aligned} \tag{13}$$

Note that the case $n = 3$ corresponds to the Cusa inequality. Obviously, Theorem C is not true for $n = 1$. Theorem C asserts that inequalities of Cusa type hold true, for every integer $n \geq 2$. Theorem C improves Theorem 3 of Ref. [4].

We get also the hyperbolic analog

Theorem D *For every integer $n \geq 1$ and $x \in (0, \infty)$, we have*

$$0 < \frac{\sinh x}{x} + \frac{\tanh x}{2x} - \frac{3}{2} < \left(\frac{\sinh x}{x}\right)^2 + \frac{\tanh x}{x} - 2 < \cdots < f_h(n,x) = \left(\frac{\sinh x}{x}\right)^n + \frac{n \tanh x}{2x} - \frac{n+2}{2}. \tag{14}$$

Theorem E *For every integer $n \geq 1$ and $x \in (0, \infty)$, we have*

$$0 < \frac{x}{\sinh x} + \frac{x}{2\tanh x} - \frac{3}{2} < \left(\frac{x}{\sinh x}\right)^2 + \frac{x}{\tanh x} - 2 < \cdots < g_h(n,x) = \left(\frac{x}{\sinh x}\right)^n + \frac{nx}{2\tanh x} - \frac{n+2}{2}. \tag{15}$$

Theorem F *For every integer $n \geq 2$ and $x \in (0, \infty)$, we have*

$$0 < \left(\frac{\sinh x}{x}\right)^2 - \frac{2\cosh x}{3} - \frac{1}{3} < \left(\frac{\sinh x}{x}\right)^3 - \cosh x < \cdots < \left(\frac{\sinh x}{x}\right)^n - \frac{n \cosh x}{3} + \frac{n-3}{3}. \tag{16}$$

Note that the case $n = 3$ corresponds to the Lazarevic inequality. However, Theorem F is not true for $n = 1$. In fact, we may prove $\left(\frac{\sinh x}{x}\right) - \frac{\cosh x}{3} - \frac{2}{3} < 0$ (to see that it suffices to calculate the second derivative of $\sinh x - \frac{x \cosh x}{3} - \frac{2x}{3}$. It equals $\frac{1}{3}(\sinh x - x\cosh x) < 0$). Theorem F asserts that inequalities of Lazarevic type hold true, for every integer $n \geq 2$.

2. Proofs

2.1 Proof of Theorem A

The first inequality of (11) has been proved by [2] for $x \in \left(0, \frac{\pi}{2}\right)$, (see (4) above)

$$\begin{gathered} \frac{\sin x}{x} + \frac{\tan x}{2x} + \frac{1}{2} < \left(\frac{\sin x}{x}\right)^2 + \frac{\tan x}{x} \Leftrightarrow \\ 0 < \frac{\sin x}{x} + \frac{\tan x}{2x} - \frac{3}{2} < \left(\frac{\sin x}{x}\right)^2 + \frac{\tan x}{x} - 2 \Leftrightarrow \\ 0 < \frac{\sin x}{x}\left[\frac{\sin x}{x} - 1\right] + \frac{\tan x}{2x} - \frac{1}{2}. \end{gathered} \tag{17}$$

We will proceed by recurrence. Suppose up to order $p \geq 1$ inequality (11) is true for $1 \leq n \leq p$. Then, we get,

$$0 < \left(\frac{\sin x}{x}\right)^{p-1} + \frac{(p-1)\tan x}{2x} - \frac{p+1}{2} < \left(\frac{\sin x}{x}\right)^{p} + \frac{p\tan x}{2x} - \frac{p+2}{2}.$$

Compute the difference

$$\left[\left(\frac{\sin x}{x}\right)^{p+1} + \frac{(p+1)\tan x}{2x} - \frac{p+3}{2}\right] - \left[\left(\frac{\sin x}{x}\right)^{p} + \frac{p\tan x}{2x} - \frac{p+2}{2}\right]$$
$$= \left(\frac{\sin x}{x}\right)^{p}\left[\frac{\sin x}{x} - 1\right] + \frac{\tan x}{2x} - \frac{1}{2}.$$

Moreover, since for $x \in \left(0, \frac{\pi}{2}\right)$, $\left(\frac{\sin x}{x}\right) < 1$ and $\left(\frac{\sin x}{x}\right)^p < \left(\frac{\sin x}{x}\right)$. Then, (17) implies

$$\left(\frac{\sin x}{x}\right)^{p}\left[\frac{\sin x}{x} - 1\right] + \frac{\tan x}{2x} - \frac{1}{2} > \left(\frac{\sin x}{x}\right)\left[\frac{\sin x}{x} - 1\right] + \frac{\tan x}{2x} - \frac{1}{2} > 0.$$

Thus, inequality (11) is verified for $p + 1$.

2.2 Proof of Theorem B

The first inequality of (12) has been proved by Ref. [2] for $x \in \left(0, \frac{\pi}{2}\right)$ (see (5) above)

$$\frac{x}{\sin x} + \frac{x}{2\tan x} + \frac{1}{2} < \left(\frac{x}{\sin x}\right)^2 + \frac{x}{\tan x} \Leftrightarrow$$
$$0 < \frac{x}{\sin x} + \frac{x}{2\tan x} - \frac{3}{2} < \left(\frac{x}{\sin x}\right)^2 + \frac{x}{\tan x} - 2 \Leftrightarrow \tag{18}$$
$$0 < \frac{x}{\sin x}\left[\frac{x}{\sin x} - 1\right] + \frac{x}{2\tan x} - \frac{1}{2}.$$

We will proceed by recurrence. Suppose up to order $p \geq 1$ inequality (12) is true for $1 \leq n \leq p$. Then, we get

$$0 < \left(\frac{x}{\sin x}\right)^{p-1} + \frac{(p-1)x}{2\tan x} - \frac{p+1}{2} < \left(\frac{x}{\sin x}\right)^{p} + \frac{px}{2\tan x} - \frac{p+2}{2}.$$

Compute the difference

$$\left(\frac{x}{\sin x}\right)^{p+1} + \frac{(p+1)x}{2\tan x} - \frac{p+3}{2} - \left(\frac{x}{\sin x}\right)^{p} + \frac{px}{2\tan x} - \frac{p+2}{2}$$
$$= \left[\frac{x}{\sin x}\right]^{p}\left[\frac{x}{\sin x} - 1\right] + \frac{x}{2\tan x} - \frac{1}{2}.$$

Moreover, since for $x \in \left(0, \frac{\pi}{2}\right)$, $\left(\frac{x}{\sin x}\right) > 1$ and $\left(\frac{x}{\sin x}\right)^p > \left(\frac{x}{\sin x}\right)$. Then, (18) implies

$$\left[\frac{x}{\sin x}\right]^{p}\left[\frac{x}{\sin x} - 1\right] + \frac{x}{2\tan x} - \frac{1}{2} > \left(\frac{x}{\sin x}\right)\left[\frac{x}{\sin x} - 1\right] + \frac{x}{2\tan x} - \frac{1}{2} > 0.$$

Thus, inequality (12) is verified for $p + 1$.

2.3 Proof of Theorem C

For the first inequality, we compute the difference

$$\left(\frac{\sin x}{x}\right)^2 - \frac{2\cos x}{3} - \frac{1}{3} - \left[\left(\frac{\sin x}{x}\right)^3 - \cos x\right]$$
$$= \left(\frac{\sin x}{x}\right)^2 \left[1 - \left(\frac{\sin x}{x}\right)\right] + \frac{\cos x - 1}{3}.$$

Moreover, for $x \in (0, \frac{\pi}{2})$, the following inequalities hold

$$1 - \frac{x^2}{6} < \frac{\sin x}{x} < 1 - \frac{x^2}{6} + \frac{x^4}{120}, \quad -\frac{x^2}{2} < \cos x - 1 < -\frac{x^2}{2} + \frac{x^4}{24}.$$

We then deduce

$$\left(\frac{\sin x}{x}\right)^2 \left[1 - \left(\frac{\sin x}{x}\right)\right] + \frac{\cos x - 1}{3} < \left[1 - \frac{x^2}{6} + \frac{x^4}{120}\right]^2 \left(\frac{x^2}{6}\right) - \frac{x^2}{6} + \frac{x^4}{72} =$$
$$-\frac{x^4}{24} + \frac{x^6}{135} - \frac{x^8}{2160} + \frac{x^{10}}{86400} = -\frac{x^4}{86400}\left(3600 - 640x^2 + 40x^4 - x^6\right) < 0, \tag{19}$$

since $(3600 - 640x^2 + 40x^4 - x^6)$ is positive and has no root for $x \in (0, \frac{\pi}{2})$. This proved the first inequality of (13).

We will proceed now by recurrence. Suppose up to order $p \geq 2$ inequality (13) is true for $1 \leq n \leq p$. Then, we get:

$$0 < \left(\frac{\sin x}{x}\right)^{p-1} - \frac{(p-1)\cos x}{3} + \frac{p-4}{3} < \left(\frac{\sin x}{x}\right)^p - \frac{p\cos x}{3} + \frac{p-3}{3}.$$

Compute the difference

$$\left(\frac{\sin x}{x}\right)^p - \frac{p\cos x}{3} + \frac{p-3}{3} - \left[\left(\frac{\sin x}{x}\right)^{p+1} - \frac{(p+1)\cos x}{3} + \frac{p-2}{3}\right]$$
$$= \left(\frac{\sin x}{x}\right)^p \left[1 - \left(\frac{\sin x}{x}\right)\right] + \frac{\cos x - 1}{3}.$$

Moreover, since for $x \in (0, \frac{\pi}{2})$, $\left(\frac{\sin x}{x}\right) < 1$ and $\left(\frac{\sin x}{x}\right)^p < \left(\frac{\sin x}{x}\right)$. Then, (19) implies

$$\left(\frac{\sin x}{x}\right)^p \left[1 - \left(\frac{\sin x}{x}\right)\right] + \frac{\cos x - 1}{3} < \left(\frac{\sin x}{x}\right)^2 \left[1 - \left(\frac{\sin x}{x}\right)\right] + \frac{\cos x - 1}{3} < 0.$$

Thus, inequality (13) is verified for $p + 1$.

2.4 Proof of Theorem D

The first inequality of (14) has been proved by [2] for $x \in (0, \infty)$ (see (7) above)

$$\begin{aligned} &\frac{\sinh x}{x} + \frac{\tanh x}{2x} + \frac{1}{2} < \left(\frac{\sinh x}{x}\right)^2 + \frac{\tanh x}{x} \Leftrightarrow \\ 0 < &\frac{\sinh x}{x} + \frac{\tanh x}{2x} - \frac{3}{2} < \left(\frac{\sinh x}{x}\right)^2 + \frac{\tanh x}{x} - 2 \Leftrightarrow \\ 0 < &\frac{\sinh x}{x}\left[\frac{\sinh x}{x} - 1\right] + \frac{\tanh x}{2x} - \frac{1}{2}. \end{aligned} \tag{20}$$

We will proceed by recurrence. Suppose up to order $p \geq 1$ inequality (14) is true for $1 \leq n \leq p$. Then, we get,

$$0 < \left(\frac{\sinh x}{x}\right)^{p-1} + \frac{(p-1)\tanh x}{2x} - \frac{p+1}{2} < \left(\frac{\sinh x}{x}\right)^{p} + \frac{p \tanh x}{2x} - \frac{p+2}{2}.$$

Compute the difference

$$\begin{aligned} &\left[\left(\frac{\sinh x}{x}\right)^{p+1} + \frac{(p+1)\tanh x}{2x} - \frac{p+3}{2}\right] - \left[\left(\frac{\sinh x}{x}\right)^{p} + \frac{p\tanh x}{2x} - \frac{p+2}{2}\right] \\ &= \left(\frac{\sinh x}{x}\right)^{p}\left[\frac{\sinh x}{x} - 1\right] + \frac{\tanh x}{2x} - \frac{1}{2}. \end{aligned}$$

Moreover, since for $x \in (0, \infty)$, $\left(\frac{\sinh x}{x}\right) > 1$ and $\left(\frac{\sinh x}{x}\right)^p > \left(\frac{\sinh x}{x}\right)$.. Then, (20) implies

$$\left(\frac{\sinh x}{x}\right)^{p}\left[\frac{\sinh x}{x} - 1\right] + \frac{\tanh x}{2x} - \frac{1}{2} > \left(\frac{\sinh x}{x}\right)\left[\frac{\sinh x}{x} - 1\right] + \frac{\tanh x}{2x} - \frac{1}{2} > 0.$$

Thus, inequality (14) is verified for $p + 1$.

2.5 Proof of Theorem E

The first inequality of (15) has been proved by [2] for $x \in (0, \infty)$ (see (7) above)

$$\begin{aligned} &\frac{x}{\sinh x} + \frac{x}{2\tanh x} + \frac{1}{2} < \left(\frac{x}{\sinh x}\right)^2 + \frac{x}{\tanh x} \Leftrightarrow \\ 0 < &\frac{x}{\sinh x} + \frac{x}{2\tanh x} - \frac{3}{2} < \left(\frac{x}{\sinh x}\right)^2 + \frac{x}{\tanh x} - 2 \Leftrightarrow \\ 0 < &\frac{x}{\sinh x}\left[\frac{x}{\sinh x} - 1\right] + \frac{x}{2\tanh x} - \frac{1}{2}. \end{aligned} \tag{21}$$

We will proceed by recurrence. Suppose up to order $p \geq 1$ inequality (15) is true for $1 \leq n \leq p$. Then, we get

$$0 < \left(\frac{x}{\sinh x}\right)^{p-1} + \frac{(p-1)x}{2\tanh x} - \frac{p+1}{2} < \left(\frac{x}{\sinh x}\right)^{p} + \frac{px}{2\tanh x} - \frac{p+2}{2}.$$

Compute the difference

$$\left(\frac{x}{\sinh x}\right)^{p+1}+\frac{(p+1)x}{2\tanh x}-\frac{p+3}{2}-\left(\frac{x}{\sinh x}\right)^{p}+\frac{px}{2\tanh x}-\frac{p+2}{2}$$
$$=\left[\frac{x}{\sinh x}\right]^{p}\left[\frac{x}{\sinh x}-1\right]+\frac{x}{2\tanh x}-\frac{1}{2}.$$

Moreover, since for $x\in(0,\infty)$, $\left(\frac{x}{\sinh x}\right)<1$ and $\left(\frac{x}{\sinh x}\right)^{p}<\left(\frac{x}{\sinh x}\right)$. Then, (21) implies

$$\left[\frac{x}{\sinh x}\right]^{p}\left[\frac{x}{\sinh x}-1\right]+\frac{x}{2\tanh x}-\frac{1}{2}>\left(\frac{x}{\sinh x}\right)\left[\frac{x}{\sinh x}-1\right]+\frac{x}{2\tanh x}-\frac{1}{2}>0.$$

Thus, inequality (15) is verified for $p+1$.

2.6 Proof of Theorem F

For the first inequality we compute the difference

$$\left(\frac{\sinh x}{x}\right)^{2}-\frac{2\cosh x}{3}-\frac{1}{3}-\left[\left(\frac{\sinh x}{x}\right)^{3}-\cosh x\right]$$
$$=\left(\frac{\sinh x}{x}\right)^{2}\left[1-\left(\frac{\sinh x}{x}\right)\right]+\frac{\cosh x-1}{3}.$$

Using the Lazarevic inequality

$$\left(\frac{\sinh x}{x}\right)^{3}>\cosh x.$$

we deduce

$$\left(\frac{\sinh x}{x}\right)^{2}\left[1-\left(\frac{\sinh x}{x}\right)\right]+\frac{\cosh x-1}{3}<\left(\frac{\sinh x}{x}\right)^{2}\left[1-\left(\frac{\sinh x}{x}\right)\right]+\frac{\left(\frac{\sinh x}{x}\right)^{3}-1}{3}$$
$$=\left(\frac{\sinh x}{x}\right)^{2}-\frac{2\left(\frac{\sinh x}{x}\right)^{3}}{3}-\frac{1}{3}=-\frac{1}{3}\left(\frac{2\sinh x}{x}+1\right)\left(\frac{\sinh x}{x}-1\right)^{2}<0.$$

for $x\in(0,\infty)$. This proved the first inequality of (16).

We will proceed now by recurrence. Suppose up to order $p\geq 2$ inequality (16) is true for $2\leq n\leq p$. Then, we get:

$$0<\left(\frac{\sinh x}{x}\right)^{p-1}-\frac{(p-1)\cosh x}{3}+\frac{p-4}{3}<\left(\frac{\sinh x}{x}\right)^{p}-\frac{p\cosh x}{3}+\frac{p-3}{3}.$$

Compute the difference

$$\left(\frac{\sinh x}{x}\right)^{p}-\frac{p\cosh x}{3}+\frac{p-3}{3}-\left[\left(\frac{\sinh x}{x}\right)^{p+1}-\frac{(p+1)\cosh x}{3}+\frac{p-2}{3}\right]$$
$$=\left(\frac{\sinh x}{x}\right)^{p}\left[1-\left(\frac{\sinh x}{x}\right)\right]+\frac{\cosh x-1}{3}.$$

Consider at first.

Lemma 2.6 Let $p \geq 2$ be an integer then the X-polynomial

$$P(X) = X^p(1-X) + \left(\frac{X^3-1}{3}\right)$$

is negative for $X \geq 0$.

Indeed,

$$\begin{aligned} P(X) &= \frac{1}{3}\left[X^p(1-X) + (X-1)\left(X^2+X+1\right)\right] \\ &= \frac{1}{3}(X-1)\left[X^2+X+1-3X^p\right] = -\frac{1}{3}(X-1)^2\left[1+2X+3X^2+3X^3+\cdots+3X^{p-1}\right]. \end{aligned}$$

Then using again the Lazarevic inequality, we derive

$$\begin{aligned} &\left(\frac{\sinh x}{x}\right)^p\left[1-\left(\frac{\sinh x}{x}\right)\right] + \frac{\cosh x - 1}{3} < \left(\frac{\sinh x}{x}\right)^p\left[1-\left(\frac{\sinh x}{x}\right)\right] + \frac{\left(\frac{\sinh x}{x}\right)^3 - 1}{3} \\ &= \frac{1}{3}\left(\left(\frac{\sinh x}{x}\right)-1\right)\left[\left(\frac{\sinh x}{x}\right)^2 + \left(\frac{\sinh x}{x}\right) + 1 - 3\left(\frac{\sinh x}{x}\right)^p\right] \\ &= -\frac{1}{3}\left(\left(\frac{\sinh x}{x}\right)-1\right)^2\left[1+2\left(\frac{\sinh x}{x}\right)+3\left(\frac{\sinh x}{x}\right)^2+3\left(\frac{\sinh x}{x}\right)^3+\cdots+\left(\frac{\sinh x}{x}\right)^{p-1}\right] < 0, \end{aligned}$$

by Lemma 2.6 where $X = \frac{\sinh x}{x}$. Thus, inequality (16) is verified for $p + 1$.

3. Further remarks

The interesting question is whether it is possible to generalize the previous chains of inequalities or to find new ones dependent on n.

Consider again inequalities chains proved by [13] (Theorem 2.1 or Theorem 4.1) for $x \in \left(0, \frac{\pi}{2}\right)$,

$$\begin{aligned} &\frac{1}{2}\left[\left(\frac{\sin x}{x}\right)^2 + \frac{\tan x}{x}\right] > \frac{1}{3}\left[\frac{2\sin x}{x} + \frac{\tan x}{x}\right] > \\ &\frac{1}{2}\left[\left(\frac{x}{\sin x}\right)^2 + \frac{x}{\tan x}\right] > \frac{1}{3}\left[\frac{2x}{\sin x} + \frac{x}{\tan x}\right] > 1 \end{aligned} \quad (22)$$

as well as [13] (Theorem 2.2 or Theorem 4.2) for $x \in (0, \infty)$,

$$\begin{aligned} &\frac{1}{2}\left[\left(\frac{\sinh x}{x}\right)^2 + \frac{\tanh x}{x}\right] > \frac{1}{3}\left[\frac{2\sinh x}{x} + \frac{\tanh x}{x}\right] > \\ &\frac{1}{2}\left[\left(\frac{x}{\sinh x}\right)^2 + \frac{x}{\tanh x}\right] > \frac{1}{3}\left[\frac{2x}{\sinh x} + \frac{x}{\tanh x}\right] > 1. \end{aligned} \quad (23)$$

We will examine the two cases separately.

3.1 Trigonometric case

Recall at first (11) and (12)

$$f(n,x) = \left(\frac{\sin x}{x}\right)^n + \frac{n\tan x}{2x} - \frac{n+2}{2}, \quad g(n,x) = \left(\frac{x}{\sin x}\right)^n + \frac{nx}{2\tan x} - \frac{n+2}{2}.$$

It is interesting to ask if we have analog chains for other values of n $\neq 1, 2$ like as those provided Theorems A,B. Unfortunately, the answer is no. We cannot provide more generalized chains. Indeed, one proved $f(1, x) - g(n, x) > 0, for\ n = 1, 2$. Otherwise, thanks to *Maple* we may also prove:

$$\begin{aligned} f(2,x) - g(n,x) &> 0, \quad \text{for} \quad n \le 3, \\ f(3,x) - g(n,x) &> 0, \quad \text{for} \quad n \le 4, \\ f(4,x) - g(n,x) &> 0, \quad \text{for} \quad n \le 5, \\ f(5,x) - g(n,x) &> 0, \quad \text{for} \quad n \le 7, \ldots. \end{aligned}$$

We may expect that

$$\begin{aligned} f(p,x) - g(n,x) &> 0, \quad \text{for} \quad 1 \le n \le p+1, \\ f(p,x) - g(n,x) &> 0, \quad \text{for} \quad 5 \le n \le p+2. \end{aligned}$$

3.2 Hyperbolic case

Recall (14) and (15)

$$f_h(n,x) = \left(\frac{\sinh x}{x}\right)^n + \frac{n\tanh x}{2x} - \frac{n+2}{x}, \quad g_h(n,x) = \left(\frac{x}{\sinh x}\right)^n + \frac{nx}{2\tanh x} - \frac{n+2}{2}.$$

In this case too unfortunately, we have not analog chains for other values of n $\neq 1$, 2 like as those provided Theorems D, E. We have only $f_h(1,x) - g_h(n, x) > 0, for\ n = 1$, 2. Otherwise, thanks to *Maple* we may prove: - the difference $fh(p, x) - gh(n, x)$ has always zero for $p = 1, 2, 3$.

However, we have

$$\begin{aligned} f_h(4,x) - g_h(n,x) &> 0, \quad \text{for} \quad n \le 6, \\ f_h(5,x) - g_h(n,x) &> 0, \quad \text{for} \quad n \le 7, \\ f_h(6,x) - g_h(n,x) &> 0, \quad \text{for} \quad n \le 8, \ldots. \end{aligned}$$

We may expect that

$$f_h(p,x) - g_h(n,x) > 0, \quad \text{for} \quad 4 \le p, \quad n \le p+2.$$

4. Concluding remarks and perspectives

Following ideas of [4] Chen and Mortici who proposed to study the above families of inequalities depending on a (positive) real parameter n in order to extend their Theorems 1, 2, 3. They proved Theorems 4, 5 as extensions of Theorems 1, 2. We may hope to replace n by real parameters for which the chains introduced in the above Theorems A–F hold true.

2010 Mathematics subject classification

26D07, 33B10, 33B20, 26D15.

Author details

Abd Raouf Chouikha
Paris-Sorbonne University, Paris-Nord, LAGA Institut Galilee, Villetaneuse, France

*Address all correspondence to: jujul53@yahoo.com

References

[1] Wilker JB. Problem E 3306. American Mathematical Monthly. 1989;**96**(1):55

[2] Chen C-P, Cheung W-S. Sharpness of Wilker and Huygens type inequalities. Journal of Inequalities and Applications. 2012;**2012**:72. DOI: 10.1186/1029-242X-2012-72

[3] Mortici C. The natural approach of Wilker-Cusa-Huygens inequalities. Mathematical Inequalities & Applications. 2011;**14**:535-541

[4] Chen C-P, Mortici C. The relationship between Huygens and Wilker inequalities and further remarks. Applicable Analysis and Discrete Mathematics. 2023;**17**:092-100

[5] Neuman E. On Wilker and Huygens type inequalities. Mathematical Inequalities & Applications. 2012;**15**(2): 271-279

[6] Wu S-H, Srivastava HM. A further refinement of Wilker's inequality. Integral Transforms and Special Functions. 2008;**19**:757-765

[7] Zhu L. On Wilker-type inequalities. Mathematical Inequalities & Applications. 2007;**10**(4):727-731

[8] Baricz A, Sandor J. Extensions of generalized Wilker inequality to Bessel functions. Journal of Mathematical Inequalities. 2008;**2**:397-406

[9] Wu S-H, Srivastava HM. A weighted and exponential generalization of Wilker's inequality and its applications. Integral Transforms and Special Functions. 2007;**18**(8):525-535

[10] Neuman E, Sandor J. On some inequalities involving trigonometric and hyperbolic functions with emphasis on the Cusa-Huygens, Wilker and Huygens inequalities. Mathematical Inequalities & Applications. 2010;**13**(4):715-723

[11] Sumner JS, Jagers AA, Vowe M, Anglesio J. Inequalities involving trigonometric functions. American Mathematical Monthly. 1991;**98**(3): 264-267

[12] Zhang L, Zhu L. A new elementary proof of Wilker's inequalities. Mathematical Inequalities & Applications. 2008;**11**:149-151

[13] Zhu L, Malesevic B. New Wilker-type and Huygens-type inequalities. Hacettepe Journal of Mathematics and Statistics. 2021;**50**(1):46-62

Chapter 5

Random Processes Defined by Stochastic Differential and Difference Equations

Pavel Loskot

Abstract

Random processes are a key component in modeling stochastic systems. They are often defined by stochastic differential or, in discrete time, difference equations (SDEs), which precisely describe how the instantaneous time-dependent and for multidimensional processes also location-dependent values vary. The solutions of SDEs are Markov processes, which is important in the analysis and simulations. The aim of this chapter is to examine various SDE models of random processes and their specific cases, for example, the random processes that arise in statistical filtering of random signals. The problem of discretizing continuous processes and linearizing nonlinear processes is also considered. Since general Langevin equation is often difficult to solve analytically, in many scenarios, it is sufficient as well as useful to solve the corresponding Fokker-Planck equation or master equation in order to obtain the time-evolving distribution of the system states. After outlining the most common random processes in continuous and discrete time such as Bernoulli and Poisson sequences, telegraph signal, and Wiener and Gaussian processes, numerical methods for solving SDEs are discussed. The chapter concludes by presenting a general method for generating random processes that are defined by their probability distribution and the auto-covariance or auto-correlation function (ACF).

Keywords: dynamic system, Fokker-Planck equation, Kalman filter, Langevin equation, master equation, stochastic differential equation, random process

1. Introduction

Random processes have been studied in different forms for decades. They are integral component of describing stochastic systems and their dynamics. They frequently appear in many applications of statistical signal processing, and they are also considered in modeling phenomena in engineering, computer science, statistical physics, social sciences, and more recently also in computational biology and medicine. Therefore, there exists very rich literature, and in many cases, also a good theoretical understanding of their models and properties. In practical settings, the choice of a random process is dictated by the specific application as well as by the tractability of mathematical analysis and feasibility of producing numerical results.

Among different models of random processes, the processes described by stochastic differential (in continuous time) or difference (in discrete time) equations (SDEs) are probably the most common. The SDE models are sufficiently versatile and in many cases offer good theoretical frameworks and efficient numerical algorithms. More importantly, the solutions of these SDEs are Markov processes, which are more prone to analysis and simulations.

This chapter explores different forms of SDEs that are used to define various random processes. It is clear that this is a very large topic with many results, which has been evolving for decades. The aim is to highlight the key ideas while the detailed description can be found in the cited literature. The advanced theoretical concepts were limited to minimum in order to make the discussion accessible for typical graduate students in engineering. The references consist only of the textbooks and monographs on stochastic processes [1–18]. In particular, the reference [4] is a good introductory textbook. The book [17] is a recommended reading to gain more advanced theoretical foundations. The fundamental concepts in statistical signal processing are provided in [14] and in estimation theory in [11]. The aspects of computer simulations involving random processes are considered in [16].

The topics that are not covered, but which may nevertheless be highly relevant to stochastic processes, include the boundary conditions, absorbing processes, the first passage time and other such metrics, many methods and software tools for numerically solving the SDEs and integro-differential equations, analytical methods for solving SDEs having a specific structure, working with SDEs involving spatial diffusion, defining and generating complex-valued random processes and other. Some examples of more recent research topics in stochastic processes that are not covered in this chapter include their use in machine learning models and algorithms, defining stochastic processes in complex topological spaces such as manifolds, stochastic processes on graphs, multivariate stochastic processes involving mixed distributions, partially defined stochastic processes and so on.

This chapter also assumes that the readers are already familiar with the basic concepts in stochastic processes such as the probability distributions of different orders, stationarity, ergodicity, definition of the ACF, Markovian property, and understand linear auto-regressive modeling of stochastic processes, and why Kalman filter has been introduced. It is an advantage to already have working knowledge of differential equations and the strategies to obtain their solutions.

The rest of this chapter is organized as follows. Section 2 outlines various linear and nonlinear SDE models in continuous and discrete time and also considers the problems of discretization and linearization. Section 3 defines the Langevin, Fokker-Planck and master equations. The common random processes are presented in Section 4. Numerical methods for solving SDEs are discussed in Section 5. Section 6 provides a general method for generating random processes with the defined distribution and the ACF. Section 7 concludes the chapter.

The following mathematical notations are used in this chapter. A scalar, vector and matrix process, respectively, is denoted as $x(t)$, $\boldsymbol{x}(t)$, and $\boldsymbol{X}(t)$, in continuous time, $t \in \mathcal{R}$, and as $x[t]$, $\boldsymbol{x}[t]$, and $\boldsymbol{X}[t]$, in discrete time, $t \in \mathbb{Z}$. The first time-derivative is denoted as $\dot{x}(t) = dx(t)/dt$, whereas the k-th derivatives, $k > 1$, are denoted as $x^{(k)}(t) = d^k x(t)/dt^k$. Other used symbols: $|\cdot|$ denotes absolute value, $E[\cdot]$ denotes expectation, $Prob\{\cdot\}$ denotes probability, $\delta(t)$ denotes Dirac delta function, the Kronecker delta function, $\delta_{ij} = 1$, if $i = j$, and 0 otherwise, $\boldsymbol{I}$ is an identity matrix, $\boldsymbol{0}$ is an all-zeros vector or matrix, $(\cdot)^T$ denotes a matrix transpose, $(\cdot)!$ is the factorial, and

$\approx$ indicates approximation. Moreover, for simplicity, all signals and values are assumed to be real-valued.

2. Modeling random processes as SDEs

Random processes can be conveniently modeled by SDEs. These models can be linear or nonlinear and defined in continuous time or in discrete time. The continuous-time nonlinear SDEs are preferred for developing theoretical foundations of stochastic processes, since they allow using differential (and integral) calculus. The discrete-time linear SDEs are normally used in generating the samples of stochastic processes in computer simulations and in implementing the methods of digital signal processing.

2.1 Linear SDE models

In continuous time, a linear random process, $x(t)$, is defined by the m-th order linear non-homogeneous differential equation,

$$\sum_{i=0}^{m} a_i(t)x^{(i)}(t) = s(t) \tag{1}$$

where $a_i(t)$ as well as $s(t)$ are other defined random processes, or $a_i(t)$ can be random constants. It is customary to assume that the driving process (input noise), $s(t)$, of model (1) is generated as a linear combination of higher-order derivatives, i.e.,

$$s(t) = \sum_{i=0}^{M} b_k(t)u^{(i)}(t) \tag{2}$$

where $b_i(t)$ and $u(t)$ are other defined random processes. Typically, $b_i(t)$ are deterministic functions or constants, whereas $u(t)$ is a stationary, zero-mean, unit-variance white noise, i.e., its ACF is $E[u(t)u(t+\tau)] = \delta(\tau)$.

In discrete time, a linear random process, $x[t]$, is defined by the m-th order linear non-homogeneous difference equation,

$$\sum_{i=0}^{m} a_i[t]x[t-i] = s[t] \tag{3}$$

with the driving (process) noise,

$$s[t] = \sum_{i=0}^{M} b_k[t]u[t-i]. \tag{4}$$

Similar assumptions about the processes or functions, $a_i[t]$, $b_i[t]$, and $u[t]$, are usually adopted as for continuous-time random processes. Since the descriptions in continuous and discrete time are nearly identical, in the sequel of this section, the expressions are mostly provided assuming continuous-time models.

It is common to express the *mth-order* linear model of a continuous-time random process as the first-order vector linear differential equation. In particular, it is straightforward to show that linear model (3) can be rewritten in the matrix form as

$$\underbrace{\begin{bmatrix} \dot{x}(t) \\ \dot{x}(t-1) \\ \vdots \\ \dot{x}(t-m+2) \\ \dot{x}(t-m+1) \end{bmatrix}}_{\dot{\boldsymbol{x}}(t)} = \underbrace{\begin{bmatrix} -a_1(t) & 1 & 0 & \cdots & 0 \\ -a_2(t) & 0 & 1 & \ddots & 0 \\ \vdots & \vdots & \ddots & \ddots & \vdots \\ -a_{m-1}(t) & 0 & 0 & \ddots & 1 \\ -a_m(t) & 0 & 0 & \cdots & 0 \end{bmatrix}}_{\boldsymbol{A}(t)} \underbrace{\begin{bmatrix} x(t) \\ x(t-1) \\ \vdots \\ x(t-m+2) \\ x(t-m+1) \end{bmatrix}}_{\boldsymbol{x}(t)} + \underbrace{\begin{bmatrix} b_0(t) \\ \vdots \\ b_M(t) \\ \vdots \\ 0 \end{bmatrix}}_{\boldsymbol{b}(t)} u(t). \tag{5}$$

In the discrete time, the equivalent first-order vector difference equation is written as

$$\boldsymbol{x}[t] = \boldsymbol{A}[t]\boldsymbol{x}[t-1] + \boldsymbol{b}[t]u[t] \tag{6}$$

assuming that the discrete-time indices, $t \in \mathbb{Z}$.

In the literature, model (5) is generalized as ([17], (1.89)),

$$\dot{\boldsymbol{x}}(t) = \mathbf{A}(t)\boldsymbol{x}(t) + \mathbf{B}(t)\dot{\mathbf{u}}(t). \tag{7}$$

Importantly, the derivatives in (7) may not be defined, if the underlying processes are not differentiable everywhere; in such a case, the differential eq. (7) must be formulated with differentials, $\mathrm{d}x(t) = x(t)\mathrm{d}t$, and, $\mathrm{d}u(t) = u(t)\,\mathrm{d}t$. Then, conditioned on matrix, $\mathbf{A}(t)$, a solution of the homogeneous equation is the matrix, $\mathbf{X}(t,s)$, such that $\frac{\partial}{\partial t}\mathbf{X}(t,s) = \mathbf{A}(t)\mathbf{X}(t,s)$ and $\mathbf{X}(s,s) = \mathbf{I}$ is an identity matrix. Denoting the initial value as $\mathbf{x}(0) = \mathbf{x}_0$, the overall solution is obtained by the integration, i.e.,

$$\mathbf{x}(t) = \mathbf{X}(t,0)\mathbf{x}_0 + \int_0^t \mathbf{X}(t,s)\mathbf{B}(s)\dot{\mathbf{u}}(s)\,\mathrm{d}s. \tag{8}$$

Note that the mean process $\mathrm{E}[\mathbf{x}(t)] = \mathbf{X}(t,0)\mathbf{x}_0$, and the mean of its derivative $\mathrm{E}[\dot{\mathbf{x}}(t)] = \frac{\mathrm{d}}{\mathrm{d}t}\mathrm{E}[\mathbf{x}(t)] = \mathbf{A}(t)\mathrm{E}[\mathbf{x}(t)]$. These solutions can be further specialized by conditioning also on the matrix, $\mathbf{B}(t)$. Thus, if matrices, $\mathbf{A}$ and $\mathbf{B}$, are time-invariant and known, the solution, $\mathbf{X}(t,s) = \exp(\mathbf{A}(t-s))$, can be substituted into Eq. (8).

Given constant matrices, $\mathbf{A}$ and $\mathbf{B}$, the SDE (7) defines different random processes for specific cases of the input process, $\mathbf{u}(t)$. In particular, provided that $\mathbf{u}(t)$ is a white Gaussian noise, the random process (8) represents a multi-dimensional Brownian motion, i.e., a stationary Gaussian process with independent increments. The Ornstein-Uhlenbeck random process is defined for $\mathbf{u}(t)$ being a Wiener process, which is a continuous Gaussian process with independent increments.

There is also an integral representation of stationary random processes in the frequency domain. It is known as the Cramér spectral representation, and it is written as the inverse Fourier transform. Thus, a random process, $x(t)$, can be generated from the random increments, $\mathrm{d}Z(\omega)$, as [7],

$$x(t) = \frac{1}{2\pi}\int_{-\infty}^{\infty} e^{j\omega t}X(\omega)\,\mathrm{d}\omega = \frac{1}{2\pi}\int_{-\infty}^{\infty} e^{j\omega t}\,\mathrm{d}Z(\omega). \tag{9}$$

The random increment process, $\mathrm{d}Z(\omega)$, has zero mean, and its ACF function defined in the frequency domain is also the spectral density, i.e., $\mathrm{E}[\mathrm{d}Z(\omega)\mathrm{d}Z(\nu)] = S(\omega)\delta(\omega - \nu)\,\mathrm{d}\omega\,\mathrm{d}\nu$.

2.2 Nonlinear SDE models

An effective way to obtain nonlinear models of random processes is to consider a nonlinear transformation, $g(x, t)$, of the linear random process, $x[t]$. Hence, define a random observation process

$$y[t] = g(x, t) + v[t] \tag{10}$$

where $v[t]$ represents a measurement noise, which is usually assumed to be zero-mean, stationary, and white.

A common strategy for processing nonlinear signals is to linearize the model about a suitable value, $x_0[t]$, at time t. This strategy is neither optimum nor the most effective, but it is often used in practice. In particular, the first-order Taylor approximation of the process model (10) is written as

$$y[t] = g(x_0, t) + \left.\frac{\mathrm{d}g(x, t)}{\mathrm{d}x}\right|_{x=x_0(t)} (x[t] - x_0[t]) + v[t]. \tag{11}$$

The value of $x_0[t]$ affects whether the linearization error could be neglected with respect to the strength of the measurement noise, $v[t]$, so it must be updated at every time instant, t. The practical choice is to set $x_0[t]$ to be the predicted value of $x[t]$ using the past estimated values, $\hat{x}(t-1), \hat{x}(t-2), \ldots$, or simply letting, $x_0[t] = \mathrm{E}[x[t]]$, if the variance, $\mathrm{var}[x[t]]$, is small.

A nonlinear form of SDE model (7) can be written as ([17], eq. (4.1)),

$$\dot{\mathbf{x}}(t) = \mathbf{a}(\mathbf{x}, t) + \mathbf{B}(\mathbf{x}, t)\dot{\mathbf{u}}(t) \tag{12}$$

where the vector function, $\mathbf{a}(\mathbf{x}, t) = [a_1(\mathbf{x}, t), a_2(\mathbf{x}, t), \ldots]^T$, and the elements of the matrix, $\mathbf{B}(\mathbf{x}, t)$, are the multivariate processes, $[\mathbf{B}(\mathbf{x}, t)]_{ij} = b_{ij}(\mathbf{x}, t)$. The corresponding stochastic integral representation is

$$\mathbf{x}(t) = \mathbf{x}(0) + \int_0^t \mathbf{a}(\mathbf{x}(s), s)\,\mathrm{d}s + \int_0^t \mathbf{B}(\mathbf{x}(s), s)\dot{\mathbf{u}}(s)\,\mathrm{d}s. \tag{13}$$

In general, integrating a random process can be performed assuming Itô, Stratonovich, backward, and other methods including a path integral ([17], Section 4.1). These methods lead to specific numerical algorithms and have different levels of convergence and stability. The choice of the appropriate method is mainly dependent on the ACF of the random process. In this chapter, the SDE models of random processes are presented assuming Itô integration (calculus).

More importantly, it can be shown that the solutions of the integral equation (13) are Markovian processes. It is then not surprising that many examples of Markovian processes can be found in the literature as well as in practical applications. Moreover, if the values of a Markov process are chosen from a discrete, countably finite, or infinite set, such a process is referred to as Markov chain. Some examples of the

Markov chain processes include a one-dimensional random walk, a queuing system, inventory modeling, branch processes, and games involving success runs [10].

A scalar Markovian process solving (13) is referred to as a diffusion process, provided that

$$\begin{aligned} \lim_{\Delta t \to 0} \frac{1}{\Delta t} \mathrm{E}[x(t+\Delta t) - x(t), x(t)] &= a(x,t) \\ \lim_{\Delta t \to 0} \frac{1}{\Delta t} \mathrm{E}\left[(x(t+\Delta t) - x(t))^2, x(t)\right] &= b^2(x,t) \end{aligned} \tag{14}$$

are continuous and deterministic processes, which are referred to as drift and diffusion coefficient, respectively. The diffusion process can be defined similarly in higher dimensions by assuming a drift vector and a diffusion matrix. Moreover, a diffusion process becomes a classical Brownian motion when it has zero drift and a constant diffusion.

2.3 Filtering random processes

Consider the random process defined by Eq. (8). Denote $\overline{\mathbf{x}}(t) = \mathbf{X}(t,0)\mathbf{x}_0$, $\mathbf{h}(t,s) = \mathbf{X}(t,s)$, and $\mathbf{B}(s)\dot{\mathbf{u}}(s) = (\mathbf{y}(s) - \overline{\mathbf{y}}(s))$, where the means $\overline{\mathbf{x}}(t) = \mathrm{E}[\mathbf{x}(t)]$ and $\overline{\mathbf{y}}(t) = \mathrm{E}[\mathbf{y}(t)]$. With these substitutions, the random process (8) can be rewritten as

$$\mathbf{x}(t) = \overline{\mathbf{x}}(t) + \int_0^t \mathbf{h}(t,s)(\mathbf{y}(s) - \overline{\mathbf{y}}(s))\,\mathrm{d}s. \tag{15}$$

Eq. (15) now represents a random process generated from another random process, $\mathbf{y}(t)$. More importantly, provided that (cf. (10)),

$$\mathbf{y}(t) = \mathbf{a}(\tilde{\mathbf{x}}, t) + \mathbf{v}(t) \tag{16}$$

the random process (15) is a linear estimate of the process, $\tilde{\mathbf{x}}(t)$, in an additive measurement noise, $\mathbf{v}(t)$, from the observations, $\mathbf{y}(t)$, using a linear and generally non-stationary filter with the impulse response, $\mathbf{h}(t,s)$. For example, the minimum mean square error (MMSE) filter must satisfy the integral equation,

$$\int_0^t \mathbf{h}(t,r)\mathbf{C}_{\mathbf{y}}(r,s)\,\mathrm{d}r = \mathbf{C}_{\mathbf{x},\mathbf{y}}(t,s), \quad \forall s \in (0,t) \tag{17}$$

where $\mathbf{C}_{\mathbf{y}}(t,s)$ is the covariance matrix of observations, $\mathbf{y}(t)$, and $\mathbf{C}_{\mathbf{x},\mathbf{y}}(t,s)$ is the matrix of cross-covariances between processes, $\mathbf{x}(t)$ and $\mathbf{y}(t)$. Analogical expressions can be also defined in the discrete time.

In the sequel of this subsection, a general model of random processes is presented that is used to obtain a discrete-time Kalman filter. The actual Kalman filter is derived, for example, in [11]. The Kalman filter is known to be the best linear unbiased estimator (BLUE) of a linear random process under these conditions:

- the observations are linear;
- the measurement noise is additive, even though possibly non-stationary;

- the random process to be estimated can be also non-stationary, but it is generated by linear filtering of a white process (driving) noise;
- the process noise, i.e., also the estimated random process and the measurement noise are uncorrelated.

Let assume the model of measurements in the form,

$$\begin{aligned}\mathbf{y}[t] &= \mathbf{D}[t]\mathbf{x}[t] + \mathbf{d}[t] + \mathbf{v}[t] \\ \mathbf{v}[t] &= \mathbf{A}_{\mathbf{v}}[t]\mathbf{v}[t-1] + \mathbf{b}_{\mathbf{v}}[t] + \mathbf{q}_{\mathbf{v}}[t]\end{aligned} \tag{18}$$

where $\mathbf{D}[t]$, $\mathbf{d}[t]$, $\mathbf{A}_{\mathbf{v}}[t]$, and $\mathbf{b}_{\mathbf{v}}[t]$ are known (deterministic) functions. The measurement noise, $\mathbf{v}[t]$, has zero mean, the covariance matrix, $\mathbf{C}_{\mathbf{v}}[t]$, and it is uncorrelated with the estimated random process, $\mathbf{x}[t]$, i.e., $\mathbf{q}_{\mathbf{v}}[t]$ is a zero-mean white noise, which is uncorrelated with the estimated process noise, $\mathbf{q}[t]$. The estimated process noise is modeled after (6), i.e.,

$$\mathbf{x}[t] = \mathbf{A}[t]\mathbf{x}[t-1] + \mathbf{b}[t] + \mathbf{q}[t] \tag{19}$$

where $\mathbf{A}[t]$ and $\mathbf{b}[t]$ are known (deterministic) functions, and $\mathbf{q}[t]$ is a zero-mean, white noise having the covariance matrix, $\mathbf{C}_{\mathbf{q}}[t]$, and it is uncorrelated with the measurement noise, $\mathbf{v}[t]$.

The correlations make the measurement noise to be predictable, so it can be added to the estimated process. The extended vector of parameters becomes

$$\begin{bmatrix}\mathbf{x}[t] \\ \mathbf{v}[t]\end{bmatrix} = \begin{bmatrix}\mathbf{A}[t] & \mathbf{0} \\ \mathbf{0} & \mathbf{A}_{\mathbf{v}}[t]\end{bmatrix}\begin{bmatrix}\mathbf{x}[t-1] \\ \mathbf{v}[t-1]\end{bmatrix} + \begin{bmatrix}\mathbf{b}[t] \\ \mathbf{b}_{\mathbf{v}}[t]\end{bmatrix} + \begin{bmatrix}\mathbf{q}[t] \\ \mathbf{q}_{\mathbf{v}}[t]\end{bmatrix} \tag{20}$$

and the corresponding measurements

$$\mathbf{y}[t] = [\mathbf{D}[t] \quad \mathbf{I}]\begin{bmatrix}\mathbf{x}[t] \\ \mathbf{v}[t]\end{bmatrix} + \mathbf{d}[t]. \tag{21}$$

The random processes (20) and (21) are then used to obtain the Kalman filter.

2.4 Discretization of continuous-time models

Digital signal processing requires representing the continuous-time random processes as discrete sequences of random samples. In addition, it is desirable that these samples are statistically uncorrelated. The procedure to obtain the uncorrelated samples is known as Karhunen-Loéve expansion in the literature. In particular, given a finite set of K orthonormal continuous real-valued functions, $\phi_k(t)$, over a finite time interval, T, such that

$$\int_T \phi_k(t)\phi_l(t)\,dt = \begin{pmatrix}1, & k = l \\ 0, & k \neq l\end{pmatrix} \tag{22}$$

the task is to decompose the random process, $x(t)$, into the sum

$$x(t) = \sum_{k=1}^{K} X_k \phi_k(t) \tag{23}$$

such that

$$\mathrm{E}[X_k X_l] = \begin{pmatrix} \lambda_k, & k = l \\ 0, & k \neq l. \end{pmatrix}. \tag{24}$$

Consequently, the mean process and the ACF, respectively, are defined as

$$\begin{aligned} \overline{x}(t) &= \mathrm{E}[x(t)] = \sum_{k=1}^{K} \mathrm{E}[X_k]\phi_k(t) \\ C_x(t,s) &= \mathrm{E}[(x(t) - \overline{x}(t))(x(s) - \overline{x}(s))] = \sum_{k=1}^{K} \lambda_k \phi_k(t)\phi_k(s). \end{aligned} \tag{25}$$

In addition to being orthonormal, the basis functions, $\phi_k(t)$, must satisfy the Fredholm integral equation,

$$\int_{\mathcal{T}} C_x(t,s)\phi_k(s)\,\mathrm{d}s = \lambda_k \phi_k(t), \quad t \in \mathcal{T}. \tag{26}$$

The Fredholm integral equations are often encountered in designing statistical signal processing methods. They are difficult to solve analytically, unless the underlying random process is stationary. In practice, it is sufficient to show that the adopted set of orthonormal functions, $\phi_k(t)$, satisfies condition (26) rather than finding the eigenvalues and the eigenfunctions of the ACF.

It should be noted that ordinary Nyquist sampling of random signals may not yield samples that are uncorrelated. In such a case, Karhunen-Loéve expansion can be used to obtain the uncorrelated samples. In such a case, the set of orthonormal functions, $\phi_k[t]$, must be chosen, so that the discrete-time ACF can be computed as

$$C_x(t,s) = \sum_{k=1}^{K} \lambda_k \phi_k[t]\phi_k[s] \tag{27}$$

for all the indices, t and s, from a finite subset of integers. Unlike in continuous time, the values, λ_k, can be computed from the variance matrix, $\mathrm{var}[\mathbf{X}] = \mathrm{E}\left[(\mathbf{X} - \overline{\mathbf{X}})(\mathbf{X} - \overline{\mathbf{X}})^T\right]$, where $\mathbf{X} = [X_1, \ldots, X_K]^T$ is a column vector of samples, and $\overline{\mathbf{X}} = \mathrm{E}[\mathbf{X}]$. It can be shown that λ_k are the roots of the characteristic polynomial defined as the determinant,

$$\det(\mathrm{var}[\mathbf{X}] - \lambda_k \mathbf{I}) = 0 \;\; \forall k. \tag{28}$$

The vectors, $\phi_k[t]$, are then computed, so they lie in the null space of the matrix, $(\mathrm{var}[\mathbf{X}] - \lambda_k \mathbf{I})$.

Furthermore, there are situations, for example, in describing the critical dynamics of a system, when the model of a stochastic process must involve both the deterministic and random effects. The random variables represent local, microscopic random fluctuations, whereas the deterministic variables model the collective, macroscopic, slowly varying effects. The corresponding SDEs are so-called Langevin equations. They are generally difficult to solve; however, the underlying probability density evolution can be often obtained by solving the corresponding Fokker-Planck equation (FPE) as will be shown in the next section.

A general Langevin equation in one dimension has the SDE form (12), i.e.,

$$\dot{x}(t) = a(x,t) + b(x,t)L(t) \tag{29}$$

where $L(t)$ represents the Langevin random force, which is assumed to be a zero-mean white Gaussian noise. If the coefficient, $b(x,t)$, does not depend on x, then the noise term in (29) is assumed to be additive; otherwise, the noise is multiplicative. The multiplicative noise allows describing more complex behaviors including non-equilibrium dynamics.

In d-dimensions, the set of general Langevin equations is defined as

$$\dot{\mathbf{x}}_i(t) = \mathbf{a}_i(\mathbf{x},t) + \mathbf{B}_{ij}(\mathbf{x},t)L_j(t), \quad i,j = 1,2, \ldots, d \tag{30}$$

where $L_j(t)$ are the zero-mean Langevin random processes having the cross-covariances, $\mathrm{E}\left[L_i(t)L_j(s)\right] = 2\delta_{ij}\delta(t-s)$.

For example, a one-dimensional zero-mean Gaussian random process with the ACF, $\mathrm{E}[x(t)x(s)] = a\exp(-a, t-s,)$, is described by the Langevin SDE,

$$\dot{x}(t) = -ax(t) + aL(t) \tag{31}$$

where $L(t)$ is a zero-mean white Gaussian noise. This random process is normally referred to as Ornstein-Uhlenbeck process. Note also that, in the limit of very large a, the process, $x(t)$, becomes white.

3. Evolution of probability density

By definition, at any given time instant, the value of a random process is a random variable, which is described by a particular probability density function (PDF). It is, therefore, of interest to investigate how such a PDF evolves in time along the realizations of a random process.

Consider a general nonlinear random process described by model (12). As stated previously, the solutions of this SDE are always Markov processes defined by their transition probability density, $p(\mathbf{x}_t, t, \mathbf{x}_s, s)$, where, for notational convenience, $\mathbf{x}_t \equiv \mathbf{x}(t)$, and, $\mathbf{x}_s \equiv \mathbf{x}(s)$. The evolution of the probability density of the random variable, $\mathbf{x}_t$, is described by the forward Kolmogorov equation, which is better known as the FPE. It assumes that $t > s$, and the initial condition $p(\mathbf{x}, s) = \delta(\mathbf{x})$. On the other hand, the evolution from the final (terminal) state, $p(\mathbf{x}, s) = u_s(\mathbf{x})$, is described by a similar partial differential equation, i.e., the backward Kolmogorov equation, assuming $t \leq s$.

The FPE can be effectively formulated using the Fokker-Planck operator. Hence, assuming the PDF, $p(\mathbf{x}, t)$, define the operator

$$L_{\mathbf{x}}p = \sum_i \frac{\partial}{\partial \mathbf{x}_i}\left(\sum_j \frac{\partial}{\partial \mathbf{x}_j}\mathbf{B}_{ij}(\mathbf{x},t)p - \mathbf{a}_i(\mathbf{x},t)p\right) \tag{32}$$

where the subscripts, i and j, denote the components of vectors or the elements of the process matrix, $\mathbf{B}$. The FPE can be then written as

$$\frac{\partial p(\mathbf{x}_t,t,\mathbf{x}_s,s)}{\partial t} = L_{\mathbf{x}_t}p(\mathbf{x}_t,t,\mathbf{x}_s,s), \quad t > s. \tag{33}$$

Note that, in the limit, $\lim_{t\to s} p(\mathbf{x}_t,t,\mathbf{x}_s,s) = \delta(\mathbf{x}_t - \mathbf{x}_s)$.

Omitting the dependence on the initial state, $\mathbf{x}_s$, at time $t = s$, the FPE of a d-dimensional diffusion process defined by the SDE model (12) is written as

$$\frac{\partial p(\mathbf{x},t)}{\partial t} = -\sum_{i=1}^{d}\frac{\partial}{\partial \mathbf{x}_i}(\mathbf{a}_i(\mathbf{x},t)p(\mathbf{x},t)) + \sum_{i,j=1}^{d}\frac{\partial^2}{\partial \mathbf{x}_i \partial \mathbf{x}_j}(D_{ij}(\mathbf{x},t)p(\mathbf{x},t)) \tag{34}$$

where $\mathbf{a}(\mathbf{x},t)$ is the drift vector, and the diffusion coefficients are computed as $D_{ij} = \frac{1}{2}\sum_{k=1}^{d}\mathbf{B}_{ik}(\mathbf{x},t)\mathbf{B}_{jk}(\mathbf{x},t)$.

The one-dimensional Ornstein-Uhlenbeck process, i.e., $\dot{x}(t) = -ax(t) + b\dot{u}(t)$, (cf. (31)) is described by the FPE,

$$\frac{\partial p(x,t)}{\partial t} = a\frac{\partial(xp(x,t))}{\partial x} + \frac{b^2}{2}\frac{\partial^2 p(x,t)}{\partial x^2}. \tag{35}$$

A Brownian motion process in one dimension is a special case of the diffusion having zero drift and the diffusion coefficient equal to 1/2. In such a case, $\dot{\mathbf{x}}(t) = \dot{\mathbf{u}}(t)$, where $\mathbf{u}(t)$ is a Wiener process, and the corresponding FPE is

$$\frac{\partial p(x,t)}{\partial t} = \frac{1}{2}\frac{\partial^2 p(x,t)}{\partial x^2}. \tag{36}$$

Assuming the initial condition, $p(x,0) = \delta(x)$, the SDE (36) has the solution, $p(x,t) = (2\pi t)^{-1/2}\exp(-x^2/(2t))$, i.e., it is a non-stationary Gaussian process.

In general, the FPE can be solved for special cases, such as when the coefficients of the SDE are time-independent. The stationary solution is obtained by assuming that $\dot{\mathbf{x}}(t) = 0$, for some $t_{ss} < t$. The solution of a non-stationary FPE can be obtained by separation or transformation of variables, variational approach, eigenvalue expansion, numerical integration, and other methods ([12], Ch. 3).

Furthermore, the dynamics of many physical and chemical systems are often described by so-called a master equation. The master equation describes the distribution of the discrete states over time. For these systems, it is desirable to model how likely the system is at any given state at different time instances. The switching between the states occurs randomly at random time instances with a certain rate. This can be described by a continuous-time Markov chain.

Specifically, the master equation defines the change of the probability distribution, $\mathbf{P}(t)$, of the system state at time, t. It is the first-order matrix SDE,

$$\dot{\mathbf{P}}(t) = \mathbf{A}(t)\mathbf{P}(t) \tag{37}$$

where $\mathbf{A}(t)$ denotes the transition matrix. Its elements, $[\mathbf{A}(t)]_{ij}$, $i \neq j$, are non-negative, whereas the diagonal elements are set, so the rows of $\mathbf{A}$ sum to zero.

The matrix, $\mathbf{A}$, is the Laplacian of a directed weighted graph representing the state transitions of a Markov chain with the weights being equal to the rates of the state transitions. In case the elements, $[\mathbf{A}(t)]_{ij}$, of the transition matrix reflect the probabilities of a homogeneous Markov chain to jump from the state, i, to the state, j, at time instant, t, then by Chapman-Kolmogorov equation,

$$\mathbf{A}(t+s) = \mathbf{A}(t)\mathbf{A}(s). \tag{38}$$

In discrete time, it follows that $\mathbf{P}(t) = \mathbf{P}^t(1)$, so the master equation can be expressed as

$$\frac{\mathrm{d}}{\mathrm{d}t}[\mathbf{P}]_i(t) = \sum_{j \neq i} \Big([\mathbf{A}]_{ij}(t)[\mathbf{P}]_j(t) - [\mathbf{A}]_{ji}(t)[\mathbf{P}]_i(t) \Big). \tag{39}$$

Importantly, this indicates that the master equation does not depend on the diagonal elements of the transition matrix, $\mathbf{A}$. At equilibrium, the detailed balance requires that

$$[\mathbf{A}]_{ij}[\mathbf{P}]_j = [\mathbf{A}]_{ji}[\mathbf{P}]_i \quad \forall i,j. \tag{40}$$

The corresponding probability distribution of states, $\mathbf{P}$, is referred to as the equilibrium distribution. The equilibrium describes the time-reversibility of microscopic dynamics, which is different from a steady-state; the latter occurs, when, $\frac{\mathrm{d}}{\mathrm{d}t}[\mathbf{P}]_i(t) = 0$, for $t > t_{\mathrm{ss}}$, and $\forall i$.

The master equation can be used to model a one-dimensional birth-death process. In particular, if the population size, $x(t)$, is of interest, it can increase by one to $x(t+s) = x(t) + 1$, due to a birth event, or decrease by one to $x(t+s) = x - 1$, when a death occurred, while $x(t) \geq 0$, for $\forall t$. Assuming that the transitions are Markovian, the time-dependent transition probabilities are defined as

$$P_{ij}(\Delta t) = \mathrm{Prob}\{x(t+\Delta t) = j, x(t) = i\}. \tag{41}$$

For small $\Delta t > 0$, and the current population size, $i \geq 0$, it can be assumed that at most one birth or death has occurred, so that,

$$\begin{aligned} P_{i,i+1} &= \alpha i \Delta t, \quad i \geq 0 \\ P_{i,i-1} &= \beta i \Delta t, \quad i \geq 1 \\ P_{i,i} &= 1 - (\alpha + \beta) i \Delta t, \quad i \geq 1. \end{aligned} \tag{42}$$

The coefficients, α and β, in (42) represent the probabilities that the corresponding events occur per unit of time. Denoting the probability distribution of the population sizes at time t as $P_i(t)$, the resulting master equation is written as

$$\begin{aligned} \frac{\mathrm{d}}{\mathrm{d}t} P_i(t) &= \alpha(i-1)P_{i-1}(t) + \beta(i+1)P_{i+1}(t) - (\alpha+\beta) i P_i(t), \quad i \geq 1 \\ \frac{\mathrm{d}}{\mathrm{d}t} P_0(t) &= \beta P_1(t). \end{aligned} \tag{43}$$

The stationary solution of (43) is obtained assuming $\frac{d}{dt}P_i(t) = 0, i \geq 0$, i.e., when $P_0 = 1$, and, $P_i = 0, i \geq 1$; in such a case, the population eventually goes extinct. On the other hand, if $P_0 < 1$, the population can either become extinct with a certain probability, or it grows without any bounds. More precisely, the derived steady-state probabilities are computed as

$$\begin{aligned} P_i &= P_0 \prod_{j=1}^{i} \frac{\alpha(j-1)}{\beta j}, \quad i \geq 1 \\ P_0 &= \left(1 + \sum_{i=1}^{\infty} \prod_{j=1}^{i} \frac{\alpha(j-1)}{\beta j}\right)^{-1}. \end{aligned} \tag{44}$$

4. Common random processes

In simulations and modeling of various systems, some random processes are encountered more often than others. The random processes that are preferred in practical applications are those that can be succinctly described, have well-defined properties, and can be readily generated or fitted to measured data. In this section, the most common random processes are outlined starting from the random processes that are defined in discrete time, which are often referred to as random sequences, before introducing the random processes defined in continuous time.

The random sequence, $\{x[0], x[1], \ldots\}$, is a martingale, if its increments are independent and have zero mean, i.e., ([18], Ch. 6)

$$\mathrm{E}[x[t], x[0], x[1], \ldots, x[t-1]] = \mathrm{E}[x[t] - x[t-1], x[0], \ldots, x[t-1]] = 0. \tag{45}$$

More generally, a sequence, $\{y[t]\}_t$, is a martingale with respect to a sequence, $\{x[t]\}_t$, provided that

$$\mathrm{E}[y[t], x[0], \ldots, x[t-1]] = y[t-1]. \tag{46}$$

For example, if the samples, $x[t]$, are drawn independently from the same probability distribution, $p(x, \theta)$, the likelihood ratio of the estimated parameter, $\hat{\theta}$, from T observed samples, is

$$\Lambda[T] = \prod_{t=1}^{T} \frac{p(x[t], \hat{\theta})}{p(x[t], \theta)}. \tag{47}$$

The mean value of the likelihood ratio conditioned on the observations is

$$\mathrm{E}[\Lambda[T], x[1], \ldots, x[T-1]] = \Lambda[T-1] \tag{48}$$

so the sequence of likelihoods is the martingale.

In continuous time, the martingale process is defined as

$$\mathrm{E}[x(t_2), x(t), t \leq t_1 < t_2] = x(t_1) \tag{49}$$

or conditioned on another process as

$$\mathrm{E}[y(t_2), x(t), t \le t_1 < t_2] = y(t_1). \tag{50}$$

The Wiener process is an example of the martingale in continuous time.

The conditional probability of samples in a Markov sequence satisfies

$$P(x[t], x[1], \ldots, x[t-1]) = P(x[t], x[t-1]). \tag{51}$$

The higher-order Markov sequences can be also defined; however, they are assumed rarely in practical problems. The Markov sequences attaining a finite set of values are often referred to as Markov chains, and their values are referred to as states.

The Markov chain is irreducible, if any state can be reached from any other state in a finite number of steps, i.e.,

$$\forall x[t_1], \;\; \exists t_2 > t_1 : \;\; P(x[t_2], x[t_1]) > 0. \tag{52}$$

Assuming Chapman-Kolmogorov equation, the transition probability over T steps is computed recursively from transition probabilities over $(T-1)$ steps as

$$P(x[T] = j, x[1] = i) = \sum_k P(x[T-1] = k, x[1] = i) P(x[T] = j, x[T-1] = k). \tag{53}$$

If the chain is homogeneous, and the one-step transition probabilities are arranged in a matrix, $\boldsymbol{P}$, then the transition probabilities after k steps are computed as $\mathbf{P}^k$.

The properties of the Markov process in continuous time are identical to the Markov chain, provided that the number of states is countably finite or infinite; such a process is referred to as a continuous-time Markov chain. For example, if the process, $x(t)$, can be constructed by independent increments, then it is the Markov process.

Bernoulli sequence is formed by binary random variables having the fixed probability of outcomes. The number of successes among a given number of trials is binomially distributed, whereas the number of trials required to achieve a given number of successes has a negative binomial distribution. Bernoulli sequence can be generalized to more than two outcomes; it is then called Bernoulli scheme sequence. These sequences can be used to define other random sequences. Consider, for example, the sum

$$x[T] = \sum_{t=1}^{T} u[t] \tag{54}$$

where $u[i] \in \{-1, +1\}$, which defines a Bernoulli random walk. It has the mean, $\mathrm{E}[x[T]] = (1-2p)^T$, which can be both increasing or decreasing over time, depending on $p = \mathrm{Prob}\{x[T] = +1\}$. The variance, $\mathrm{var}[x[T]] = 4p(1-p)T$, is always increasing over time. The ACF can be derived as $\mathrm{E}[x[T_1]x[T_2]] = 4p(1-p)\min(T_1, T_2) + (1-2p)^2 T_1 T_2$. It should be noted that the random walk can be also created assuming a birth-death process discussed above.

The case, $u[i] \in \{0, 1\}$, in (54) defines a binomial counting sequence with the mean value, $\mathrm{E}[x[T]] = pT$, and the variance, $\mathrm{var}[x[T]] = p(1-p)T$. The ACF is now obtained as $\mathrm{E}[x[T_1]x[T_2]] = p(1-p)\min(T_1, T_2) + p^2 T_1 T_2$.

The binomial counting process can be generalized as a continuous-time Poisson counting process having the independent and stationary increments, and the initial value $x(0) = 0$. In the literature, these processes are sometimes referred to as renewal processes [10]. The Poisson counting process has the probability of $k \geq 0$ successes occurring over a time duration, $T > 0$, approximated by the Poisson distribution, i.e.,

$$\text{Prob}\{x(T) = k\} \approx \frac{(\lambda T)^k}{k!} \exp(-\lambda T) \tag{55}$$

where λ denotes the average rate of successes per unit time. If λ is time-dependent, such a process is called non-homogeneous. The inter-arrival time between two consecutive successes is a random variable, which can be shown to be exponentially distributed with the same parameter, λ. The inter-arrival time can be used to obtain the distribution of times until the occurrence of the k-th success; this is an Erlang random variable. The ACF of the Poisson process can be shown to be $\text{E}[x(T_1)x(T_2)] = \lambda \min(T_1, T_2) + \lambda^2 T_1 T_2$.

Poisson process is an example of a general class of Lévy random processes. Another example of the Lévy random process is a gamma process having the inter-arrival times being gamma distributed. Poisson process can be generalized as Hawkes random process. It is a marked point process, which models the random intensity changes in the arrival times as a self-excitation phenomenon ([2], Ch. 11).

The random telegraph signal, $y(t)$, can be obtained as a transformation of the Poisson process, $x(t)$, i.e.,

$$y(t) = (-1)^{x(t)} = \begin{cases} +1, & x(t) - \text{even} \\ -1, & x(t) - \text{odd}. \end{cases} \tag{56}$$

Thus, $y(t)$ is a continuous-time Markov jump process having only two states. The probability of states can be derived to be

$$\begin{aligned} \text{Prob}\{y(t) = +1\} &= \exp(-\lambda t)\cosh(\lambda t) \\ \text{Prob}\{y(t) = -1\} &= \exp(-\lambda t)\sinh(\lambda t). \end{aligned} \tag{57}$$

Note that the rate constant, λ, could be assumed to be different in the transitions to $+1$ and -1 value, respectively. The probability distribution of $y(t)$ is

$$p(y,t) = \exp(-\lambda t)(\cosh(\lambda t)\delta(y-1) + \sinh(\lambda t)\delta(y+1)) \tag{58}$$

with the mean, $\text{E}[y(t)] = \exp(-2\lambda t)$, and the variance, $\text{var}[y(t)] = 1 - \exp(-4\lambda t)$. Moreover, the telegraph signal can be randomized by assuming the product, $Uy(t)$, where U are independent and equally likely values, $+1$ or -1, generated whenever the process, $y(t)$, changes its value.

The Wiener process is best known as a model of Brownian motion of particles in a fluid. It is a solution of the second-order partial differential equation

$$\frac{\partial}{\partial t} p(x,t) = \alpha \frac{\partial^2}{\partial x^2} p(x,t), \quad x(0) = 0 \tag{59}$$

where α denotes the rate of particle collisions. Solving (59), $p(x,t)$ is the Gaussian distribution with zero mean and the variance equal to (αt), i.e., this process is non-stationary. The ACF is derived as $\text{E}[x(t_1)x(t_2)] = \alpha \min(t_1, t_2)$. More generally, the

Wiener process can be also defined assuming the time increments rather than the absolute times.

A multivariate Gaussian process is probably the most frequently assumed random process. Since these processes have been extensively described and studied in the literature, they are mentioned only very briefly here. The Gaussian process is fully defined by the vector of means and the covariance matrix; the covariance matrix also defines the spatial ACF of this process. The Gaussian distribution has the largest entropy (i.e., it is the worst-case noise) among all continuous distributions. Its widespread occurrence in many practical scenarios and systems is justified by the central limit theorem. It is also the only distribution, which is preserved by linear transformations, and for which uncorrelated variables are equivalent to independent variables. Gaussian processes play an important role in estimating the parameter values. The Gaussian mixture models add another level of flexibility in modeling random processes and in defining the prior and posterior distributions in Bayesian as well as non-Bayesian estimation of parameter values.

More complicated random processes can be built from other random processes. For example, Archimedean survival process is a vector of differences between gamma bridge processes, which are themselves created by scaling the gamma random processes by other random variables ([2], Ch. 10).

5. Numerical methods for solving SDEs

The random processes considered in this chapter are defined by the SDEs. Since many practical SDEs cannot be solved analytically, they must be solved numerically by computer simulations. The caveat is that the existing algorithms for solving ordinary differential equations (ODEs) may not be directly applicable or efficient for solving SDEs. The notable exception is SDEs with the driving noise that is generated independently of the random process values; for these processes, the algorithms developed for ODEs can be directly used for SDEs.

In general, the algorithms for solving SDEs should provide fast convergence, good accuracy, and also stability. The accuracy is affected by discretization, whereas the lack of stability may cause a sudden divergence of computations. Therefore, numerical solvers for SDEs require formal mathematical frameworks and derivations in order to satisfy these requirements.

As an example, consider the integral form of a one-dimensional time-homogeneous SDE

$$x(t) = x(t_0) + \int_{t_0}^{t} a(x(s))\,\mathrm{d}s + \int_{t_0}^{t} b(x(s))\,\mathrm{d}u(s). \tag{60}$$

Using Itô's formula, the Euler method approximates integral equation (60) as

$$x(t) \approx x(t_0) + a(x(t_0))(t - t_0) + b(x(t_0))(u(t) - u(t_0)). \tag{61}$$

The more accurate higher-order approximation can be obtained in the form

$$x(t) \approx x(t_0) + a(x(t_0))(t - t_0) + b(x(t_0)) \int_{t_0}^{t} \mathrm{d}u(s) + L_1 b(x(t_0)) \int_{t_0}^{t} \int_{t_0}^{s} \mathrm{d}u(s')\,\mathrm{d}u(s) \tag{62}$$

where the function operator, L_1, is introduced to denote $L_1 f(t) = b\frac{d}{dt}f(t)$.

Assuming the time discretization to evaluate the process, $x(t)$, at N discrete-time instances, $t = i\Delta t$, $i = 0, 1, \dots, N$, so that, $N\Delta t = T$, and denoting the Wiener process increments as $\Delta u_i = u((i+1)\Delta t) - u(i\Delta t)$, the Euler algorithm computes one of the following iterations depending on the assumed approximation, i.e.,

$$x_{i+1} = x_i + a(x_i)\Delta t + b(x_i)\Delta u_i$$
$$x_{i+1} = x_i + a(x_i)\Delta t + b(x_i)\Delta u_i + \frac{1}{2}L_0 b(x_i)\left(\Delta u_i^2 - \Delta t\right) \tag{63}$$

where the function operator, L_0, is defined as $L_0 f(t) = a\frac{\mathrm{d}}{\mathrm{d}t}f(t) + \frac{1}{2}b^2\frac{\mathrm{d}^2}{\mathrm{d}t^2}f(t)$. A better stability can be obtained by assuming $a(x_{i+1})$ and $b(x_{i+1})$, or, $(a(x_i) + a(x_{i+1}))/2$ and $(b(x_i) + b(x_{i+1}))/2$, in (63). However, these latter values do not guarantee the convergence to the correct continuous-time solution even when the time step, Δt, goes to zero. The converge problem can be rectified by using $a(\overline{x}_i)$ and $b(\overline{x}_i)$ in (63), where the filtered sequence, $\overline{x}_i = \epsilon x_{i+1} + (1-\epsilon)x_i$. For $\epsilon = 1/2$, the algorithm to generate the samples, x_i, of the random process must periodically find the root, $\overline{x}_i$, of the equation

$$2(\overline{x}_i - x_i) = a(\overline{x}_i)\Delta t + b(\overline{x}_i)\Delta u_i. \tag{64}$$

The root mean square error as a measure of the algorithm convergence between the approximately computed values, x_i, and the exact values, $x(i\Delta t)$, is of the order between $\sqrt{\Delta t}$ and Δt. Thus, the approximation accuracy improves by reducing the discretization step size. There are other algorithms, for example, Milstein algorithm, that were proposed in the literature to improve the accuracy.

There is a notion of communicative and non-communicative noises, depending whether the driving noise (usually a Wiener process with independent Gaussian increments) is additive or multiplicative, i.e., whether the scaling coefficient of the noise is independent of the random process values or not. This is important, for example, when deriving the FPE for a Langevin equation. If the noise is additive, then Itô and Stratonovich interpretation of Langevin equation leads to the same FPE; this is not the case when the noise is multiplicative.

Furthermore, similar discretization methods can be used to generate samples of the vector random processes as explained in ([5], Section 10.5). Subsequently, the vector counterparts of the Euler and Milstein algorithms exist.

In addition to low-order approximations by the Euler and Milstein algorithms, other algorithms relying on higher-order approximations are available. However, the increased accuracy of these algorithms usually comes at the cost of increased computational complexity and possible issues with convergence. In general, a good strategy is to exploit the structure of the specific SDE in order to avoid many of the computational problems. For example, the noise can be quantized to a small number of levels or even be generated as a binary sequence of ± 1 values.

The substantial computational problems arise in simulating spatially resolved partial SDEs, since they have to be discretized not only in time, but also in 2D or even 3D space. This may prevent considering any higher-order approximations and the corresponding algorithms. In the literature, the algorithms for spatial SDEs assume, for example, the fast Fourier transforms, and there is also the interaction picture method inspired by Hamiltonians in quantum mechanics.

5.1 Example

Consider the one-dimensional SDE,

$$dx(t) = \mu x(t)dt + \sigma x(t)dw(t), \quad x(0) = x_0 \tag{65}$$

with the constant drift, μ, and the constant diffusion, σ, driven by the Wiener process, $w(t)$. In this case, the solution can be obtained in the closed form, i.e.,

$$x(t) = x_0 e^{(\mu - \sigma^2/2)t + \sigma w(t)} \tag{66}$$

which can be verified by substituting into (65) and using the Itô calculus.

The exact solution (66) can be approximated by computing the approximate values, $\tilde{x}(t_i) \equiv \tilde{x}_i$, of $x(t_i)$, at chosen discrete-time instances, t_i. Specifically, using the Euler algorithm

$$\tilde{x}_i = \tilde{x}_{i-1} + \mu\tilde{x}_{i-1}\Delta t_i + \sigma\tilde{x}_{i-1}\Delta w_i, \quad \tilde{x}_0 = x_0. \tag{67}$$

The samples of the Wiener process increments are generated, $\Delta w_i = \mathcal{N}(0,1)\sqrt{\Delta t_i}$, where the time increments, $\Delta t_i = t_i - t_{i-1}$, and $\mathcal{N}(0,1)$ is the zero-mean, unit-variance Gaussian random variable.

The Milstein algorithm approximates the SDE (65) as

$$\tilde{x}_i = \tilde{x}_{i-1} + \mu\tilde{x}_{i-1}\Delta t_i + \sigma\tilde{x}_{i-1}\Delta w_i + \frac{\sigma}{2}\left(\Delta w_i^2 - \Delta t_i\right), \quad \tilde{x}_0 = x_0 \tag{68}$$

so it introduces the extra term compared to the approximation (66).

It can be shown that both Euler and Milstein algorithms converge in the mean to the exact solution as the step size, Δt, is reduced, i.e.,

$$\lim_{\Delta t \to 0} \mathrm{E}[x(t) - \tilde{x}(t)] = \mathcal{O}((\Delta t)^n) \quad \forall t > 0 \tag{69}$$

where n represents the order of converge. For L random realizations of the values, $\tilde{x}(t)$, the expectation can be evaluated as

$$\mathrm{E}[x(t) - \tilde{x}(t)] \approx \mathrm{E}[x(t)] - \frac{1}{L}\sum_{l=1}^{L}\tilde{x}_{(l)}(t). \tag{70}$$

The order, n, is $1/2$, for the Euler algorithm, and 1, for the Milstein algorithm, respectively. Consequently, in order to reduce the approximation error to one half, the step size, Δt, must be reduced to $1/4$, for the Euler algorithm, but only to $1/2$, for the Milstein algorithm.

The approximations (67) and (68) of the exact solution (66) are numerically validated in **Figure 1** (top) assuming the initial value, $x_0 = 10.0$, the parameters, $\mu = 1.0$, and, $\sigma = 0.5$, and $N = 50$ time steps in the interval $(0, 1)$. The relative approximation error is expressed as

$$\epsilon(t_i) = (100\%) \times (x(t_i) - \tilde{x}(t_i))/x(t_i). \tag{71}$$

In addition, **Figure 1** (bottom) shows the absolute mean error, $|x(t_i) - \tilde{x}(t_i)|$, as a function of the number of time steps, $N = 2^k$, $k = 2, 3, \ldots, 10$, in the interval, $(0, 1)$,

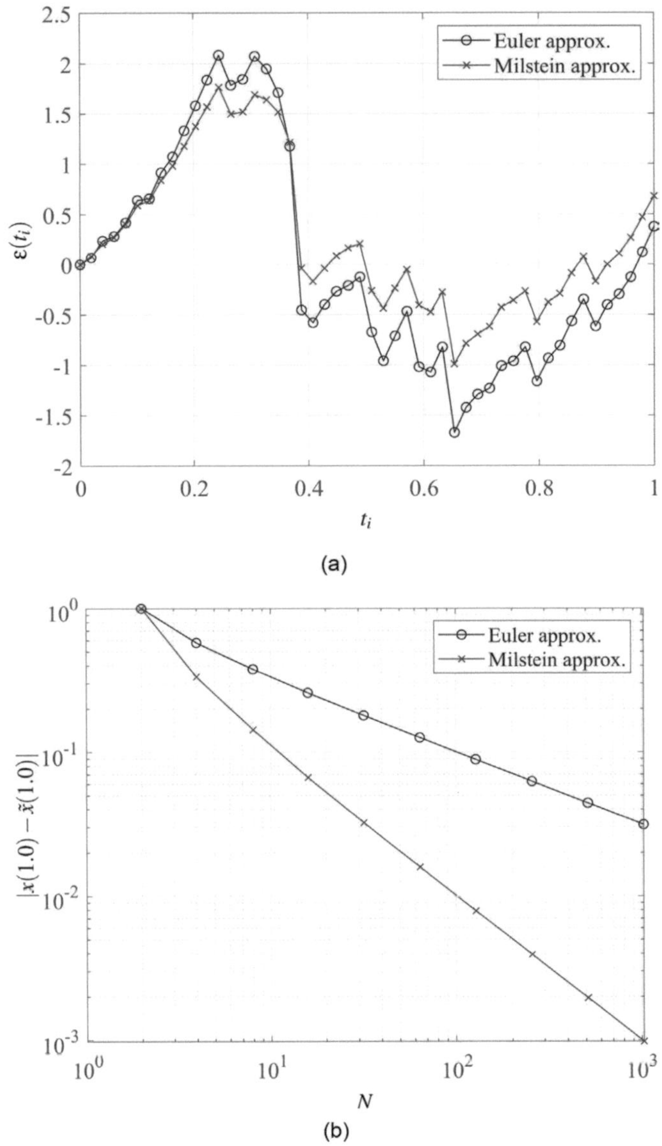

Figure 1.
Sample realization of the random process (65) and its Euler and Milstein approximations (top), and the absolute mean errors at $t_i = t_N = 1.0$ as a function of the time steps, N (bottom).

for $t_i = t_N = 1.0$. These curves indicate that the absolute mean error decreases as $(1/N)^{1/2}$, for the Euler algorithm, and as $(1/N)$, for the Milstein algorithm.

6. Generating random processes

The previous section discussed how to simulate random processes that are defined by a given SDE. This section considers the problem of generating random processes of given properties, i.e., the problem how to find the corresponding SDE model that can be used to generate samples of the random process.

In general, in most practical scenarios, the random process is typically described by the probability distribution of its samples, which also fully defines all statistical moments at any given time instant, and by the second-order pairwise moments between the samples at any two time instances; these moments are referred to as the ACF or auto-covariance function.

More importantly, the generated random processes are ergodic and stationary, so that the statistical mean is equal to the average value in time, i.e.,

$$\mathrm{E}[x(t)] = \mathrm{Av}[x(t)] = \mathrm{Av}[\mathrm{E}[x(t)]] = \mathrm{E}[\mathrm{Av}[x(t)]] \ \forall t. \tag{72}$$

The non-ergodic processes are rarely encountered in practical applications. The non-stationary process, $x(t)$, can be generated from a stationary process, $u(t)$, using the transformation involving deterministic functions, $a(t)$ and $b(t)$, as

$$x(t) = a(t)u(t) + b(t). \tag{73}$$

Note that transformation (73) is nonlinear, unless $b(t) = 0$, for $\forall t$. Moreover, the robust signal processing can be achieved by assuming the values, $\mathrm{Av}[\mathrm{E}[x(t)]]$ or $\mathrm{E}[\mathrm{Av}[x(t)]]$, instead of $\mathrm{Av}[x(t)]$ or $\mathrm{E}[x(t)]$.

The simplest, but very often considered random process is a correlated (colored) Gaussian noise. In continuous time, the uncorrelated (white) Gaussian process, $u(t)$, is correlated by a linear, not necessarily stationary filter with the impulse response, $h(t,s)$, i.e.,

$$x(t) = \int_{-\infty}^{\infty} h(t,s)u(s)\,\mathrm{d}s. \tag{74}$$

The mean and the ACF of the process, $x(t)$, can be computed as

$$\begin{aligned} \overline{x} &= \overline{u}\int_{-\infty}^{\infty} h(t,s)\,\mathrm{d}s \\ \mathrm{E}[x(t)x(s)] &= \int_{-\infty}^{\infty} h(t,r)h(s,r)\,\mathrm{d}r \end{aligned} \tag{75}$$

where $\overline{u} = \mathrm{E}[u(t)]$, and $\mathrm{E}[u(t)u(s)] = \delta(t-s)$.

Assuming a vector of mutually uncorrelated Gaussian processes, $\mathbf{u}(t) = [u_1(t), u_2(t), \dots]^T$, where each $u_i(t)$ can be individually correlated in time, can be transformed into a vector of mutually correlated processes, $\mathbf{x}(t)$, by a linear transformation

$$\mathbf{x}(t) = \mathbf{A}\mathbf{u}(t). \tag{76}$$

Then, the correlation matrix $\mathrm{E}\left[\mathbf{x}(t)\mathbf{x}^T(t)\right] = \mathbf{A}\mathrm{E}\left[\mathbf{u}(t)\mathbf{u}^T(t)\right]\mathbf{A}^T$. If the number of processes, N, is large, the elements of $\mathbf{A}$ can be efficiently calculated as

$$\begin{aligned} A_{1,1} &= \sqrt{C_{1,1}},\ A_{k,1} = \frac{C_{k,1}}{A_{1,1}},\ k = 2, \dots, N \\ A_{j,j} &= \sqrt{C_{j,j} - \sum_{i=1}^{j-1} A_{j,i}^2},\ A_{k,j} = \frac{C_{k,j} - \sum_{i=1}^{j-1} A_{k,i}A_{j,i}}{A_{j,j}},\ k = j+1, \dots, N \\ A_{N,N} &= \sqrt{C_{N,N} - \sum_{i=1}^{N-1} A_{N,i}^2} \end{aligned} \tag{77}$$

assuming, for simplicity, that all $u_i(t)$ have zero mean, and $C_{i,j} = \mathrm{E}[x_i(t)x_j(t)]$ denote the desired pairwise correlations. This procedure can be also used for a discrete-time signal represented by a column vector, $\mathbf{u}$. For very large, $N \gg 1$, the auto-regressive moving average (ARMA) model in continuous [cf. (1)] or discrete time should be used. The initial values of the generated random process can be discarded until the process becomes stationary. Alternatively, a non-stationary ARMA model can be used initially before switching to model (77) in order to speed up the convergence to stationary samples.

The above methods involving linear filtering are well justified when the samples are Gaussian. There are, however, many situations when the random process is specified by a general probability distribution and its ACF. This is not a complete statistical description, so different generation methods can yield different higher-order moments. The most straightforward, however, in practice rather complicated method is to generate uncorrelated samples with a certain distribution, so that linear filtering of these samples yields both the desired distribution as well as the ACF.

A much more tractable method first generates Gaussian samples with given correlations and then uses a memoryless nonlinear transformation to obtain the desired distribution and the ACF. In particular, let the zero-mean Gaussian noise, $u(t)$, have the ACF, $C_u(t_1-t_2) = \mathrm{E}[u(t_1)u(t_2)]$, and the pairwise PDF, $p_u(u_1,u_2,t_1-t_2)$. The random process, $x(t) = g(u(t))$, has the one-dimensional and two-dimensional PDF, respectively, [14].

$$
\begin{aligned}
p_x(x) &= \frac{p_u(g^{-1}(x))}{|\dot{g}(g^{-1}(x))|} \\
p_x(x_1,x_2) &= p_u(g^{-1}(u_1),g^{-1}(u_2))\left|\frac{dg^{-1}(u_1)}{du_1}\frac{dg^{-1}(u_2)}{du_2}\right|.
\end{aligned}
\tag{78}
$$

The corresponding mean and the ACF, respectively, can be computed as

$$
\begin{aligned}
\overline{x} &= \int_{-\infty}^{\infty} g(u)p_u(u)\,du \\
C_x(t_1-t_2) &= \int_{-\infty}^{\infty}\int_{-\infty}^{\infty} g(u_1)g(u_2)p_u(u_1,u_2,t_1,t_2)\,du_1du_2.
\end{aligned}
\tag{79}
$$

The generation procedure then proceeds in these steps:

1. find a nonlinearity, $g(\cdot)$, so that for the target output distribution, the input distribution is Gaussian;

2. given $g(\cdot)$, find the correlations (covariances), $C_u(t_1-t_2)$, so that the output process, $x(t)$, has the desired ACF, $C_x(t_1-t_2)$;

3. given $C_u(t_1-t_2)$, obtain a linear filter to generate such an ACF from the uncorrelated Gaussian samples.

This procedure is general and can be used to generate different processes with given distribution and ACF. However, in some cases, when the nature of a random process has been motivated by a specific physical or other phenomenon, it can directly indicate how to generate the underlying process. For example, a continuous-time

Poisson process can be generated by a random sequence of Dirac delta pulses with exponentially distributed inter-arrival times, which are then filtered with an integrator. It is, therefore, advisable, to check the relevant literature whether this might be the case for a given random process.

6.1 Example

Consider the problem of generating a zero-mean stationary binary random sequence, $x[t]$, of ± 1 values with a given ACF. Such a process can be generated, for example, from a discrete-time Gaussian process, $y[t]$, using the nonlinearity,

$$x[t] = \text{sign}(y[t]) = \begin{cases} +1, & y[t] \geq 0 \\ -1, & y[t] < 0 \end{cases}. \tag{80}$$

The ACF, $C_x[\tau]$, of the output process, $x[t]$, can be expressed in terms of the ACF, $C_y[\tau]$, of the input process, $y[t]$, as

$$C_x[\tau] = \frac{2}{\pi} \arcsin\left(\frac{C_y[\tau]}{C_y[0]}\right). \tag{81}$$

For example, assume that $C_x[0] = 1$, $C_x[-1] = C_x[+1] = -1/3$, and $C_x[\tau] = 0$, otherwise. In such a case, the sequence, $y[t]$, has a zero mean and the unit variance, and by inverting the ACF (81), the required ACF is $C_y[0] = 1$, $C_y[-1] = C_y[+1] = -1/2$, and $C_y[\tau] = 0$, otherwise. The Gaussian process with this ACF can be obtained by filtering the uncorrelated Gaussian samples, $u[t]$, with a discrete-time linear filter having the impulse response, $h[0] = 1/\sqrt{2}$, $h[1] = -1/\sqrt{2}$, and $h[t] = 0$, otherwise. Therefore, the process, $x[t]$, with the desired ACF is generated from the uncorrelated Gaussian samples as

$$x[t] = \text{sign}\left(\frac{u[t] - u[t-1]}{\sqrt{2}}\right). \tag{82}$$

7. Conclusions

This chapter discussed random processes that are usually modeled as SDEs. The resulting SDEs can be linear or nonlinear and defined in continuous time or discrete time. The higher-order differential and difference linear equations can be equivalently represented by the first-order vector equations. Brownian motion and Ornstein-Uhlenbeck random processes are the special cases of a linear SDE. There is also Cramér integral representation of random processes in frequency domain. The nonlinear models can be obtained by introducing a nonlinear measurement equation with added measurement noise.

Filtering and estimating random processes often give rise to random processes defined by integral equations. Langevin equation allows incorporating both deterministic and random effects. In practical applications, it is usually easier to solve the corresponding Fokker-Planck equation and obtain the time-evolution of the state distribution. In modeling physical and chemical system dynamics, the FPE is referred to as master equation.

Acknowledgements

This research was funded by a research grant from Zhejiang University.

Abbreviations

ACF	auto-correlation function
ARMA	auto-regressive moving average
BLUE	best linear unbiased estimator
FPE	Fokker-Planck equation
MMSE	minimum mean square error
ODE	ordinary differential equation
PDF	probability density function
SDE	stochastic differential equation

Author details

Pavel Loskot
ZJU-UIUC Institute, Haining, Zhejiang, China

*Address all correspondence to: pavelloskot@intl.zju.edu.cn

References

[1] Amir A. Thinking Probabilistically, Stochastic Processes, Disordered Systems, and Their Applications. Cambridge, UK: Cambridge University Press; 2021

[2] Bielecki TR, Jakubowski J, Niewęgłowski M. Structured Dependence between Stochastic Processes. Cambridge, UK: Cambridge University Press; 2020

[3] Leon-Garcia A. Probability and Random Processes for Electrical Engineering. 2nd ed. New York, USA: Addison-Wesley; 1994

[4] Gardner WA. Introduction to Random Processes With Applications. 2nd ed. New York, USA: McGraw-Hill; 1990

[5] Gardiner CW. Handbook of Stochastic Methods for Physics, Chemistry and the Natural Sciences. 3rd ed. New York, NY: Springer; 2004

[6] Grimmett GR, Stirzaker DR. Probability and Random Processes. 3rd ed. Oxford, UK: Oxford University Press; 2001

[7] Haykin S. Adaptive Filter Theory. 5th ed. Harlow, UK: Pearson Education Limited; 2014

[8] Jazwinski AH. Stochastic Processes and Filtering Theory. New York, USA: Academic Press; 1970

[9] van Kampen NG. Stochastic Processes in Physics and Chemistry. 3rd ed. Amsterdam, Netherlands: Elsevier; 2007

[10] Karlin S, Taylor HM. A First Course Instochastic Processes. 2nd ed. New York, USA: Academic Press Inc.; 1975

[11] Kay SM. Fundamentals of Statistical Signal Processing: Estimation Theory. Vol. I. Upper Saddle River, New Jersey: Prentice Hall; 1993

[12] Kwok SF. Langevin and Fokker-Planck Equations and their Generalizations. Singapore: World Scientific Publishing Co. Pte. Ltd.; 2018

[13] Miller SL, Childers D. Probability and Random Processes With Applications to Signal Processing and Communications. 2nd ed. Waltham, MA, USA: Academic Press; 2012

[14] Papoulis A, Pillai SU. Probability, Random Variables, and Stochastic Processes. 4th ed. New York, NY: McGraw-Hill; 2002

[15] Pavliotis GA. Stochastic Processes and Applications. New York, USA: Springer Science+Business Media; 2014

[16] Ross SM. Stochastic Processes. 2nd ed. New York, USA: Wiley; 1996

[17] Schuss Z. Theory and Applications of Stochastic Processes, An Analytical Approach. New York, NY: Springer; 2010

[18] Shynk JJ. Probability, Random Variables and Random Processes. Hoboken, New Jersey: John Wiley & Sons; 2013

Chapter 6

The Optimization Problems and Modeling the Radiation Characteristics of Focusing Radiating Array

Mykhaylo Andriychuk and Victor Tkachuk

Abstract

The variational statement of an optimization problem for a 3D linear array, which forms radiation in a far zone, with the subsequent application of the optimization procedure consisting of the application of a gradient method of successive approximation to its solving is examined in chapter. The linear array consists of the source of excitation, the inclined semitransparent plane mirrors, and the final metallic mirror. The quasioptical condition is applicable to the geometry of the array. The distance between the adjacent elements of the array satisfies the conditions of the Fresnel zone, and its radiation pattern (RP) is determined in a far zone. We use an assumption of separation of the variables in the planes of mirrors and the RPs in the far zone. The close formulas are got for the field in the mirrors of the array and the generated RP. The numerical computations demonstrate a rapid convergence of the used iterative method and the possibility of the array to form the radiation characteristics satisfying the different demands.

Keywords: radiating and focusing array, semitransparent mirror, quasioptical condition, transmission and reflection coefficients, RP, method of successive approximations, computational modeling

1. Introduction

While solving the electromagnetic (EM) problems of radiated and communications, plasma research, and material processing, the quasioptical condition is one of the effective tools to make the scattering problem and solve the respective optimization problems. The geometrical theory of diffraction (GTD) is basis of such a condition, and its application easily reduces the solutions to the problem of EM wave scattering when the size of the object under study is large compared to the wavelength. This a topic has been studied comprehensively over the several last decades (see monographs [1–3] and journal papers [4–6]).

The quasioptical methods were used effectively for research of the active and passive quasioptical elements [7], satellite radars [8], mirror antennas [9], parabolic antennas [10], and the development of aperture antennas [11] starting with the 90es of the last century. Despite the fact that quasioptical conditions are effective mainly for the GHz and MHz frequencies, it effectively applied recently for studying the systems in a THz frequency [12, 13].

Usually, numerical approaches are involved in solving synthetic problems. For example, the computations were used effectively for solving the quasioptical antenna systems in the range of millimeter waves [14], and frequency analysis of the EM fields in the mirror antennas [15].

The use of quasioptical conditions is one of the effective instruments that allow the simplifying of the near/far fields of antennas and as a result solves a majority of practical problems of designing the antennas and arrays of the different types. The quasioptical approach was implemented successfully to create the desired RP using the transmitting quasioptical line [16, 17], and to form the EM field of desired property by a system of the phase correctors [18].

Generally, the explored array consists of $L \times N$ mirrors and composes a plane array [17]. We explore here a separate element, which is a set of semitransparent inclined mirrors, and we show that it can form the radiation with a desired characteristic in a far zone. This approach is a generalization of that considered in Ref. [19] in the case of forming the RPs in 3D space.

We investigate in this chapter a quasioptical linear multi-element array that is excited by an antenna source (see **Figure 1**) [16]. This array can be considered in two modifications, the first one is a transmitting system in the antenna-rectenna utilization [20], and the second one is a linear array, which forms the EM field with the given RP [21]. In the latter case, it is considered a linear array focusing the EM field in a fixed area of the Fresnel zone. At such considerations, one can consider several inverse optimization problems, and consider this array as a single antenna [22]. Here, the optimization problem, in which the module of RP is given as input information, is formulated and solved using the variational formulation.

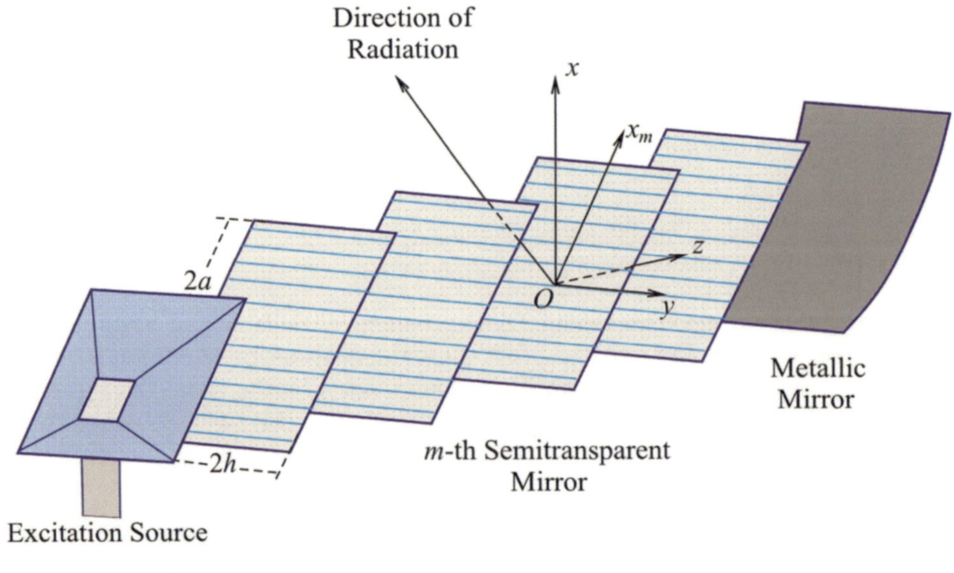

Figure 1.
The array of inclined mirrors with exciting and opaque elements.

2. The geometry of array element

2.1 The preliminary data

The definitive relations for the EM fields on the constituent elements of the array are derived in this section. The radiating vertical aperture D_0 at the beginning of the array, the parallel inclined semitransparent mirrors D_m, $m = 1, \dots, M - 1$, and the least inclined opaque mirror D_M compose an array (see **Figure 1**). The semitransparent elements transfer the input field partially, and they radiate it partially into a region, which is defined by the inclination of the elements. The radiated (reflected) and transmitted fields become the phase correction, which is defined by the array geometry and the radiation frequency. The last element reflects the incoming field fully and influences its phase only.

In order to simplify the problem, we admit that all mirrors are selfsame with the vertical length equal to $2a$, and the distance between the mirror's centers is equal to d. For space to create a given beam of the given RP, the inclination angle β in the vertical plane is given in conformity with the dimensional values a, d of mirror:

$$\sin(2\beta) = 2a/d. \tag{1}$$

The transmission T_m and reflection R_m coefficients, as well as the initial phase correction ψ_0 are related to the x_m coordinate. They are sought for, when the optimization problems are solved. In our consideration, the initial field U_0 in the element D_0 can be either prescribed or sought for.

The geometry of the array corresponds to the quasioptical conditions (2.7) (see Ref. [23]), this implies that the size of the element is larger in comparison to the length of the wave. Moreover, the distances between the adjacent mirrors are larger than the length of the wave as well. The large values of parameters ka, d/a are in the same

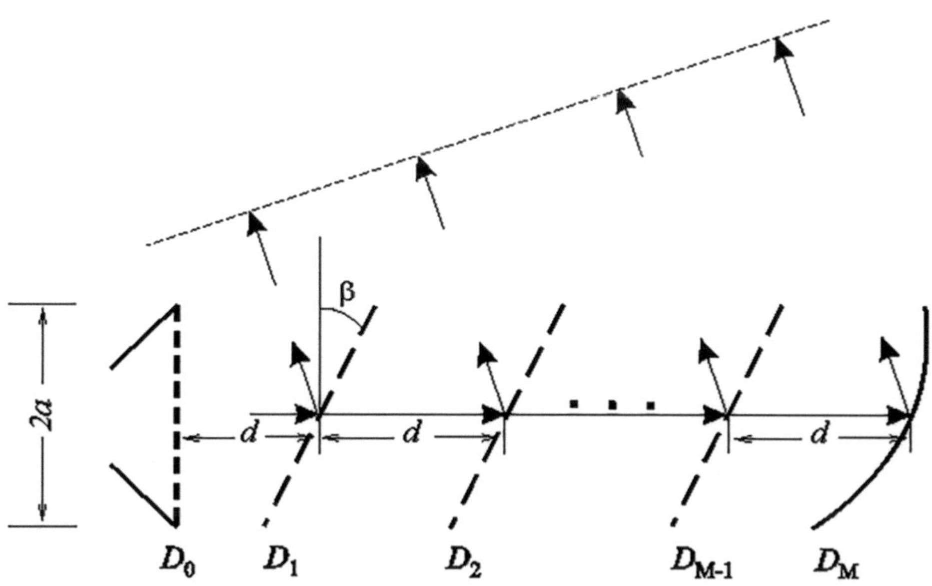

Figure 2.
Forming the EM field characteristics in the vertical plane.

order. The relation (1) defines that angle β is quite small, that is, it is inverse order to ka or d/a.

Define by $U_m, m = 0, \dots, M$, the field values in the left-hand side of the mirrors D_m (we do not take into account the phase corrections here). The phase coefficient $\exp(i\psi_0)$ the first element D_0 is included in the field U_0. The complex-valued reflection $R_m, m = 1, \dots, M$, and transmission $T_m, m = 0, \dots, M-1$, coefficients creating the fields $U_m\left(\vec{R}_m\right), m = 1, \dots, M$, are used if we calculate the transmitted and reflected fields; in general, these coefficients are not constant functions of variable x_m. One should note that vector $\vec{R}_m$ differs on the scalar value of R_m.

2.2 The field in the elements of array

We apply formula (2.1) ([22], p. 11) for the calculation of the fields in the vertical cross-section to calculate the field of the array consisting of the inclined mirrors. The explanation of the process of forming the radiation in this plane is shown in **Figure 2**.

The formula for recalculation of the fields on the two adjacent arbitrarily oriented mirrors is

$$U_{m+1}\left(\vec{R}_{m+1}\right) = \frac{k}{2\pi}\iint_{D_m} \frac{\exp\left(-ik\left|\vec{R}_m - \vec{R}_{m+1}\right|\right)}{\left|\vec{R}_m - \vec{R}_{m+1}\right|} \times U_m\left(\vec{R}_m\right)T_m\left(\vec{R}_{m-1}\right)d\vec{R}_m, \tag{2}$$

$\vec{R}_m$, $\vec{R}_{m+1}$ are 3D radius-vectors of the points in apertures D_m and D_{m+1} with the respective coordinates x_m and x_{m+1}. This formula can be simplified when using the quasioptical condition. To do this, we present the distance between points in D_m and D_{m+1} in form.

$$\left|\vec{R}_m - \vec{R}_{m+1}\right| = \sqrt{\left|\vec{r}_{m,x} - \vec{r}_{m+1,x}\right|^2 + \left(z_m - z_{m+1}\right)^2}, \tag{3}$$

$\vec{r}_{m,x}$, $\vec{r}_{m+1,x}$ are 2D vectors, and correspond to the projection points onto the vertical planes, which cross the centers of mirrors, that why.

$$\vec{R}_m = \vec{r}_{m,x} + \vec{z}_m, .\vec{R}_{m+1} = \vec{r}_{m+1,x} + \vec{z}_{m+1} \tag{4}$$

Owing to the smallness of value a/d, and Relation (1), one can simplify the denominator in Formula (2) using the value d instead of. Nevertheless, we should determine (4) more precisely in the numerator, where it is included in the function "exp". On the other hand

$$z_{m+1} - z_m = d + \left(x_{m+1}\tan\beta_{m+1} - x_m\tan\beta_m\right) \tag{5}$$

owing to the fact that the mirrors are inclined in the plane xOz. We limit ourselves to the same angles β_m and β_{m+1} of inclination of the mirrors. As a result, we get

$$|\vec{R}_m - \vec{R}_{m+1}| = d + \frac{|r_{m,x} - r_{m+1,x}|^2}{2d} + x_{m+1}\tan\beta_{m+1} - x_m \tan\beta_m, \tag{6}$$

if to take the above assumption and to take into account Tailor's expansion of the first two terms only.

We get

$$\begin{aligned} U_{m+1}\left(\vec{R}_{m+1}\right) &= \frac{k\exp(-ikd)}{2\pi\cos\beta_m} \iint\limits_{D_m} \frac{\exp\left(-ik|\vec{R}_m - \vec{R}_{m+1}|\right)}{2d} \times \\ &\exp\left(x_{m+1}\tan\beta_{m+1} - x_m\tan\beta_m\right)\times \\ &U_m\left(\vec{R}_m\right)T_m\left(\vec{R}_{m-1}\right)d\vec{R}_m, m = 0, 1, \dots, M-1 \end{aligned} \tag{7}$$

substituting (6) in (2), using the new integration variable $\vec{r}_m$ and known formula $d\vec{R}_m = (\cos\beta)^{-1}d\vec{r}_m$,

In (7), the integration domain D_m is created as a projection of D_m onto the vertical plane, angle $\beta_0 = 0$, angles $\beta_m = \beta, m = 1, \dots, M$.

The array total field is determined as a sum of fields (7) and that formed by the array of linear antennas. Consequently, the total field in the $m+1-$ th mirror has a form

$$\overline{U}_{m+1}\left(\vec{R}_{m+1}\right) = U_{LA}U_{m+1}\left(\vec{R}_{m+1}\right), m = 0, 1, \dots, M-1, \tag{8}$$

and U_{LA} denotes the field created by the array of linear antennas in the horizontal plane. We suppose here that the linear antennas are identical with the length equal to $2h$.

3. Derivation of array RP and optimization

In this section, we derive the explicit formula for the total RP of the array taking into account the properties of reflected and transmitted fields in the array elements and consider three optimization problems, which can be stated when the specific engineering demands are imposed on the RP or other radiation performances of the array.

3.1 The RP calculation

Define by x_m (x_m/a) the $m-$ th mirror coordinate. It is an independent variable of functions in the elements $D_m, m = 0, \dots, M$, and the vertical length of all mirrors is equal to $2a$.

Formula (7) for recalculation of the fields in two adjacent mirrors in the 3D case using (8) becomes

$$\begin{aligned} &\overline{u}_{m+1}(x_{m+1}, y) = B_m[u_m T_m] \equiv U_{LA}(y)\sqrt{\frac{c}{2\pi}}e^{-ikax_{m+1}\tan\beta_{m+1}}\times \\ &\int_{-1}^{1} u_m(x_m)T_m(x_m)e^{\left(-i\left[(c/2)(x_{m+1}-x_m)^2 - kax_m\tan\beta_m\right]\right)}dx_m \\ &m = 0, 1, \dots, M-1, \end{aligned} \tag{9}$$

where $U_{LA}(y)$ is the field created by a linear array in a horizontal plane, function $T_m(x_m)$ corresponds to the transmission coefficient of m-th mirror; the parameter

$$c = ka^2/d. \tag{10}$$

In Formula (9), B_m is some linear bounded operator. Formula (9) is convenient to get the representation of joint operator $\overline{A}_m^*$, which is applied for the derivation of the gradient of the respective functionals [22].

The total RP of the array is given as a sum of partial RPs of separate elements

$$f(\theta, \varphi) = \sum_{m=1}^{M} f_m(\theta, \varphi), m = 1, 2, \ldots, M, \tag{11}$$

angle θ is given in the counter-clockwise direction from the reflected field, angle φ belongs to the interval $[-\pi/2, \pi/2]$. Using the above, we calculate the partial RPs $f_m(\theta)$ by the values $U_m(x_m)$ and the parameters R_m:

$$f_m(\theta, \varphi) = B[uR] := f_{LA}(\varphi) \exp(-i(m-1)kd\cos\gamma) \times \int_{-1}^{1} R_m(x_m) u_m(x_m) \exp(-ikax_m(\tan\beta\cos\gamma - \sin\gamma))dx_m, \quad m = 1, 2, \ldots, M \tag{12}$$

$f_{LA}(\varphi)$ is the linear array RP; $\gamma = 2\beta + \theta$; (we omit constant multiplier in formula (12)).

3.2 The optimization problems

In a set of values ka, kd, c, and β, which are contained in formulas (9) and (12), we have only two independent physical values. The above is owing that the values ka and kd are calculated by c and β

$$ka = 2c/\sin(2\beta), \tag{13}$$

$$kd = 4c/\sin^2(2\beta) \tag{14}$$

(see Ref. [24]).

The optimization problems for the array under consideration can be separated into two independent problems in vertical and horizontal planes by our assumptions. Since the horizontal RP is determined by the array of linear antennas, the length of linear antennas can be the optimization parameter. Therefore, we have a set of optimization parameters in the vertical plane.

One can consider three optimization problems for such consideration.

Problem 1.

To maximize the functional

$$\kappa_1(U_0, R_1, \ldots R_M, T_1, \ldots T_{M-1}) = \frac{\|f\|^2}{\|U_0\|^2} \tag{15}$$

with the given input field U_0, the reflection coefficients $R_m, m = 1, \ldots, M$, the transmission coefficients $T_m, m = 0, \ldots, M-1$, which met the condition

$$|R_m|^2 + |T_m|^2 = 1, \tag{16}$$

and are sought for. The value of functional κ_1 is different from that of the power radiated to the prescribed angle domain, and this difference is characterized by some constant before the formula for the RP f.

The phase characteristic $\psi_0(x_0)$ does not considered here as an optimizing function. This function can be considered for optimization if a more general problem when U_0 is given as the optimizing function.

Problem 2.

This problem is related to forming the given amplitude RP $F(\theta)$, where $\theta \in [-\theta_0, \theta_0]$ (the field $U_0(x_0), x_0 \in [-1,1]$ in the input element is fixed) choosing the optimal complex-valued transmission $T_m, m = 0, \dots, M-1$ and the reflection $R_m, m = 1, \dots, M$ coefficients. Both the set of these coefficients satisfy the demands stated in Ref. [22].

The system under consideration is interpreted in Ref. [16] as a short-periodical array. By this condition, the values $R_m(x_m)$ and $T_m(x_m)$ are determined by the geometry of the array; additionally, some restrictions can be applied depending on the specific of the optimization problem.
The functional

$$\kappa_2(R_1, R_2, \dots, R_M; T_0, T_1, \dots T_{M-1}) = \int_{-\theta_0}^{\theta_0} |f(\theta)| F(\theta) d\theta \tag{17}$$

is maximized to solve Problem 2. We introduce the specific angular coordinate $\xi = \sin\theta / \sin\theta_0$ instead of the angular coordinate θ while computations. To simplify the calculations, we suppose that the given functions $U_0(x_0)$ and $F(\xi)$ satisfy the condition of normalization [25].

$$\int_{-1}^{1} U_0^2(x_0) dx_0 = 1, \quad \int_{-1}^{1} F^2(\xi) d\xi = 1 \tag{18}$$

Problem 3.

We prescribe the amplitude RP $F(\theta)$, $\theta \in [-\theta_0, \theta_0]$, one needs to determine the input field U_0, the optimal transmission $T_m(x_m)$, $m = 0, 1, \dots, M-1$ and reflection $R_m(x_m)$, $m = 1, \dots, M$ coefficients, satisfying (16), which provide the minimum for the functional

$$\sigma(U_0, R_1, \dots, R_M, T_0, \dots, T_{M-1}) = \| |f| - F \|^2 \tag{19}$$

with the constraint

$$\|U_0\| \le C, \tag{20}$$

and C is given constant. In some optimization problems, if the function U_0 is given, the last restriction is not used.

4. Numerical optimization

The numerical solving of the problems of maximization of functionals κ_1, κ_2 and minimization of functional σ is carried out by the gradient method of successive approximations. For example, the formula for the calculation of the coefficients R_m is.

$$R_m^{(n+1)} = R_m^{(n)} + \delta^{(n)} z_m^{(n)}, , m = 1, \dots, M \tag{21}$$

where $(n+1)$ and (n) are the numbers of iterations, $z_m^{(n)}$ is the gradient of function to be minimized with respect to parameter R_m in the $n-$ th step, and $\delta^{(n)}$ is chosen in such a way that the value of the respective functional is decreased/increased. As the numerical computations show, the iterative process is quickly convergent, and usually one needs 10–15 iterations in order to attain an accuracy of not less than 1%. We consider below the examples of solving the optimization problems (15) and (17) for the different problem parameters and estimate the effectiveness from the point of view of the convergence effectiveness and attaining the better values of the explored parameters, which are subject to optimization. In our consideration, there are the complex-valued reflection coefficients $R_m(x_m), m = 1, \dots, M$, and transmission coefficients $T_m(x_m), m = 0, \dots, M-1$.

4.1 Optimization in the vertical plane

We provide firstly the computational results related to the comparison of the effectiveness of creating the prescribed characteristics of EM field radiation in the vertical plane. The array consisting of the four elements with the exciting aperture is considered (see **Figure 2**). The distance d between adjacent elements is equal to 30.81 cm, and the distance from the exciting element to the first mirror is equal to $d/2$. As the numerical calculations show, a decrease in distance from the exciting source to the first inclined element improves the effectiveness of the synthesis that resulting in increase in the value of the optimizing functional. The angle of inclination $\beta = 12^0$, the

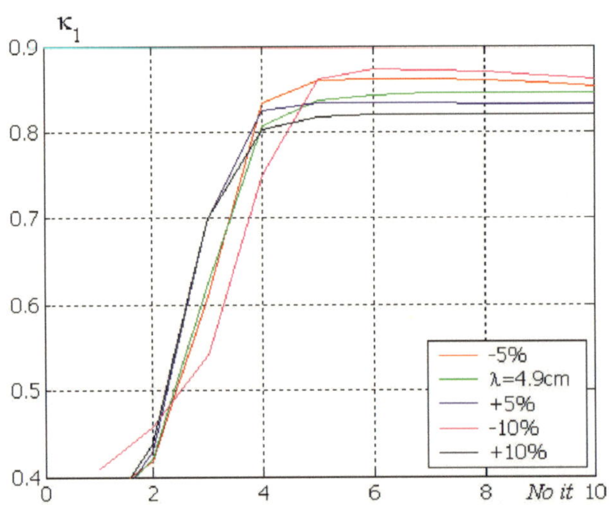

Figure 3.
The values of κ_1 functional at the different λ for Problem 1.

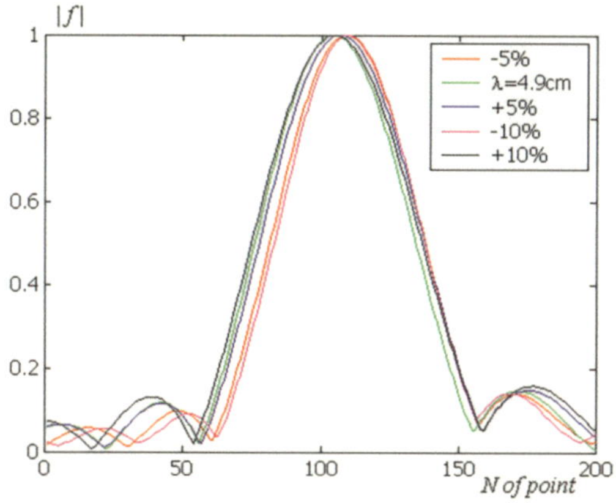

Figure 4.
The optimal amplitude RPs at the different λ for Problem 1.

length of the mirror $l = 6.0$ cm, and the length of the wave of radiation is 4.9 cm (the frequency f is equal to 5.88 GHz).

The results in **Figure 3** concern Problem 1 and show the dependence of values of functional (15) on the length λ of excitation wave. The values of κ_1 are measured along the $y-$ axis, and the number of iterations is marked along the $x-$ axis. The calculation was carried out for the central length of 4.9 cm and values in the distance $\pm 5\%$ and $\pm 10\%$ from the central value. The obtained results demonstrate the close values for all examined lengths. From the physical point of view such performance of κ_1 demonstrates the broadband of the considered array, namely the effectiveness of synthesis (solving the optimization problem) is applicable for all the considered values of λ.

The results presenting the created (synthesized) amplitude RPs for the central length of wave $\lambda = 4.9$ cm is shown in **Figure 4**. Similarly to **Figure 3**, the results are shown for five values of the length of the wave. One can see that the performances of the created amplitude DP are close in the main lobe and the difference is observed in the area of sidelobes. Totally, the level of sidelobes does not exceed 0.12 which corresponds to -18.42 dB, which is applicable for many engineering applications. The optimal amplitudes of reflection coefficients R_n are shown in **Figure 5**.

For the comparison with the previous results, the data related to solving Problem 2 are shown in **Figures 6** and **7**. The calculations are carried out for the prescribed amplitude RP

$$F(\theta) = |\cos(\theta)/\theta|, \; -\pi/2 \leq \theta \leq \pi/2. \qquad (22)$$

The values of functional (17) are shown at the same values of λ in **Figure 6**. It is observed that the optimization problem for this case provides worse results in comparison with solving Problem 1. The maximal attained values of κ_2 is equal to 0.51 in comparison with κ_1 =-.93 in the previous case. The above has a certain physical sense because the requirement to create the amplitude RP as soon as close to the required one is weaker in relation to ensuring the best power characteristics of the radiation. The created amplitude RPs for Problem 2 are shown in **Figure 6**. The numerical results demonstrate that the grade of approximation to the given amplitude RP $F(\theta)$ is

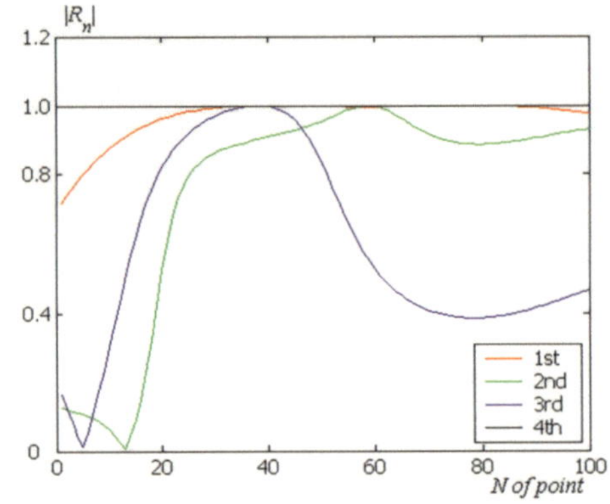

Figure 5.
The optimal amplitudes of reflection coefficients R_n for Problem 1.

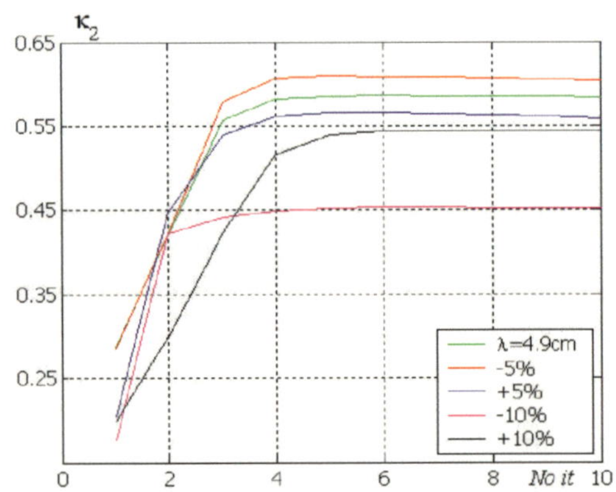

Figure 6.
The values of κ_2 functional at the different λ for Problem 2.

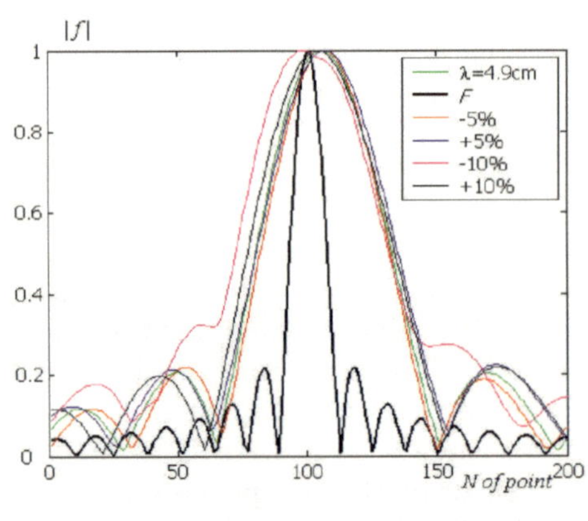

Figure 7.
The optimal amplitude RPs at the different λ for Problem 2.

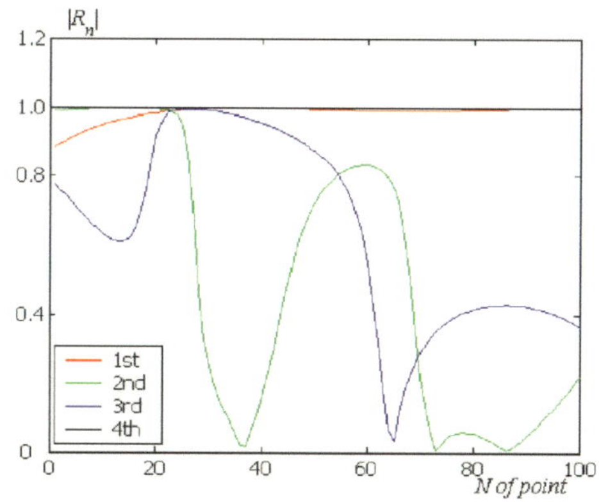

Figure 8.
The optimal amplitudes of reflection coefficients R_n for Problem 2.

different for the different values of λ. This qualitative characteristic is also worse than in the previous case. The obtained numerical results have some physical explanation because the grade of approximation to the given amplitude RP $F(\theta)$ depends on the length of wave radiation at the fixed values of size $2a$ of the mirror in the horizontal plane. The optimal amplitudes of reflection coefficients R_n are shown in **Figure 8**.

4.2 3D optimization

The presented results are related to solving the optimization Problem 2, which consists of functional (17) maximization. The given results of optimization demonstrate the possibility of creating the various RPs that depend on the array's parameters, namely the size of elements, their quantity, and radiation frequency are considered to be optimized. The reflection $R_m(x_m)$ and transmission $T_m(x_m)$ coefficients are prescribed as the constant values. The mirrors are inclined to the vertical plane with the angle $\beta = 15^0$. The length of elements $2a = 0.25\,\text{m}$ in vertical plane, $h = a$, and h is horizontal size; and the wavenumber $k = 0.61\,\text{m}^{-1}$ (the wavelength $\lambda = 10.2$ m). The distance d is determined by (1); at the given a and β it is equal to 0.5 m. The horizontal RP (along y axis) is determined as the RP of the linear antenna array with the length in λ.

The data in **Figure 9** show the optimal amplitude RP of the five-element array. The value $T_m = 0.75$ ($R_m = 0.66$ for such T_m). The horizontal array size $2h$ is equal to $2/3\lambda$. The optimal RP in the $\theta-$ plane is less wide than in the $\varphi-$ plane at the chosen parameters of the array. The RP in the $\theta-$ plane becomes the first sidelobe -20 dB, the level of sidelobes decreases to -34 dB for the angles considered. The RP in the $\varphi-$ plane decreases from its maximum to the level of -23 dB. The optimal amplitude RP demonstrates that the radiation for the non-visible angles is large, this confirms the considerable reactivity of the array.

The results in **Figure 10** are shown for the array with the element length equal to λ. One can see that the horizontal main lobe changes too much at such a size as a mirror. The main lobe of the array is two-directional; by this, the first sidelobe exists with -26 dB.

The radiation property of planes $\varphi = \pi$ and $\theta = 0$ is shown in **Figure 11**. The vertical amplitude RP is red. Its form tends to be formed by the linear antenna of the equivalent length at such size of the mirror; by this, the sidelobe level decreases as for

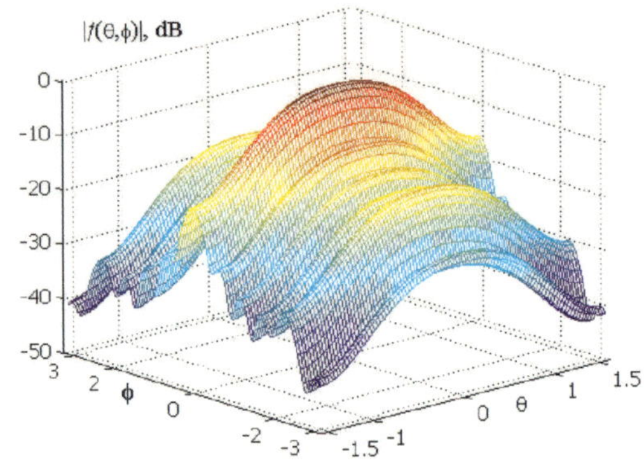

Figure 9.
The optimal amplitude RP for five-element arrays at the horizontal size $2h = 2/3\lambda$.

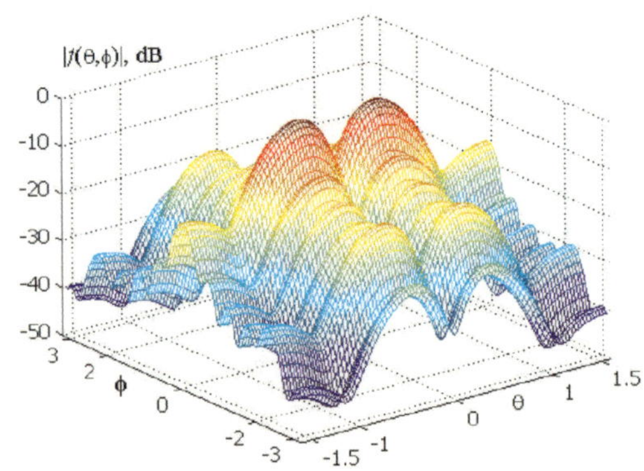

Figure 10.
The optimal amplitude RP for five-element array at the horizontal size $2h = \lambda$.

the linear antenna. Horizontal RPs are in green and blue color. The data show if the size of linear antenna tends to λ, the gap appears in the main lobe of amplitude RP. Therefore, creating the horizontal RP needs the solve the optimization problem to achieve its satisfactory characteristic in the horizontal plane.

The obtained data testify that to get the RPs closer to the desired amplitude RP one should deal with optimization for the $y-$ direction. To this, we apply the approach for creating the linear array RPs [23]. In **Figure 12**, the 3D array RP as a result of optimization of the $xOz-$ plane is demonstrated. The total 3D RP becomes a narrow main lobe; by this, the first side lobe is less than -17 dB. The sidelobes in the $\theta = 0-$ plane is less than -18 dB. Such parameters are applicable to a series of engineering demands. Evidently, the RP properties in this plane can be made better after solving the optimization problem, in which the coefficients R_m and T_m are optimizing.

The data in **Figure 13** show that the RP characteristics depend to a great extent on the quantity of the array mirrors. The data are given for the 10-mirror array. The sidelobes (including the first ones) diminish to a great extent, but the far sidelobe -15 dB in $\theta = 0-$ plane; the first sidelobe -18 dB in the $\varphi = 0-$ plane appears.

The main lobe at such a quantity of mirrors is wider. The computations show that better characteristics of the total RP can be achieved when using the additional optimization with respect to coefficients R_m and T_m. The simplest way is the increase

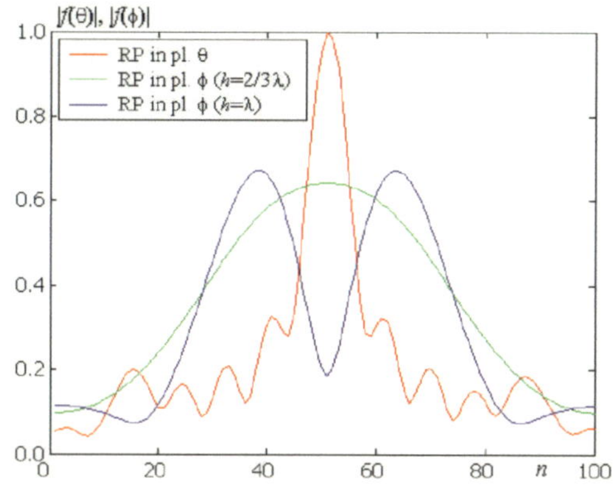

Figure 11.
The amplitude RPs for the different length h in the y− plane.

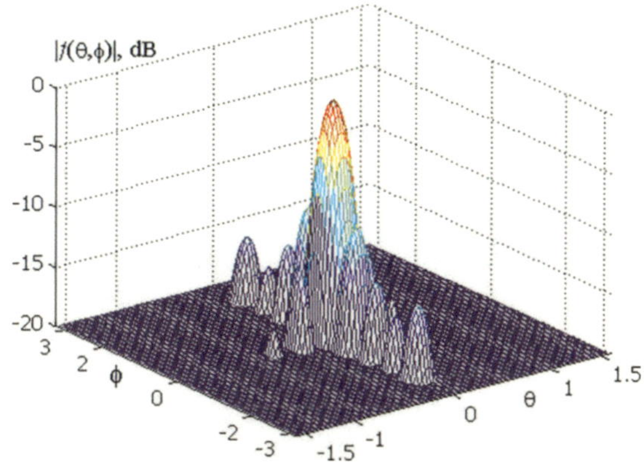

Figure 12.
The five-element array optimized amplitude RP in the y− plane.

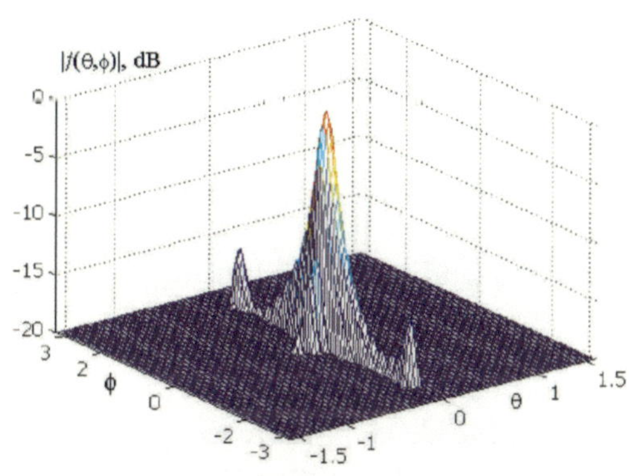

Figure 13.
The 10-element arrays optimized amplitude RP in the y− plane.

the coefficients T_m at the beginning of the array; by this, the coefficients R_m are decreasing. The above results in decreasing the main lobe width, diminution of sidelobes, as well as in the speed of their increasing.

5. Conclusions

The radiation of the linear array consisting of the semitransparent inclined mirrors has been studied in terms of improving the created amplitude RPs. The background of the approach is the strict formulation of the 3D electrodynamical problem for such an array. The analytical formulas for the field distribution in the elements of the array and RP of the whole array were obtained. The optimization problems were formulated using the variational approach that allows to reduce the explicit formulas for the gradient of the used functional and to apply successfully for the determination of the optimizing parameters the iterative method of the successive approximations. As a rule, to achieve the required exactness of calculation in several percent, we need 10–20 iterations. The calculations have been demonstrated that the radiation characteristics of RP, such as the main lobe width and the sidelobe level, depend on the array parameter, namely the transmission and reflection coefficients, the RP of the separate mirror, and its geometry, to a great extent. The above confirms the necessity of the optimization to achieve the optimal values of the above parameters allowing to form the amplitude RPs satisfying the required demands.

The consideration of the optimization problems for the reflection R_m and transmission T_m coefficients, and the geometrical parameters of the array, which provide the desired characteristics of the RPs is the perspective of the approach proposed.

Conflict of interest

Authors declare no conflict of interest.

Author details

Mykhaylo Andriychuk[1,2]* and Victor Tkachuk[1,2]

1 Pidstryhach Institute for Applied Problems of Mechanics and Mathematics, NASU, Lviv, Ukraine

2 Lviv Polytechnic National University, Lviv, Ukraine

*Address all correspondence to: andr@iapmm.lviv.ua

References

[1] Paknys R. Uniform theory of diffraction. In: Applied Frequency-Domain Electromagnetics. New York: IEEE; 2016. pp. 268-316. DOI: 10.1002/9781119127444

[2] Osipov AV, Tretyakov SA. Modern Electromagnetic Scattering Theory with Applications. Chichester, West Sussex: John Wiley & Sons; 2013. p. 824

[3] Apaydin G, Sevgi L. Electromagnetic Diffraction Modeling and Simulation with MATLAB. Norwood, MA: Artech House; 2021. p. 209

[4] Keller JB. Geometrical theory of diffraction. Journal of the Optical Society of America. 1962;**52**(2):116-130

[5] Becker A, Hansen V. A hybrid method combining the multitemporal resolution time-domain method of moments with the time-domain geometrical theory of diffraction for thin-wire antenna problems. IEEE Transactions on Antennas and Propagation. 2006;**54**(3):953-960. DOI: 10.1109/TAP.2006.869906

[6] Veruttipong TW. Time domain version of the uniform GTD. IEEE Transactions on Antennas and Propagation. 1990;**38**(11):1757-1764. DOI: 10.1109/8.102736

[7] York RA, Popovic ZB. Active and Quasi–Optical Arrays for Solid–State Power Combining. London, Boston, New York: John Wiley & Sons; 1997. p. 526

[8] Loo PK, Goussetis G. Asymmetrical impedance inverter for quasi-optical bandpass filters with transmission lines of fixed length. IEEE Transactions on Microwave Theory and Techniques. 2018;**66**(11):4794-4802. DOI: 10.1109/TMTT.2018.2873396

[9] Neilson J. Final Report Advanced Quasioptical Launcher System. San Mateo, CA, USA: Calabazas Creek Research, Inc., US; 2010. p. 11

[10] Robustillo P, Córcoles J, Rubio J. Expedited amplitude and phase tolerance analysis of reflector antenna systems with vector spherical waves. IEEE Transactions on Antennas and Propagation. 2023;**71**(1):1071-1074. DOI: 10.1109/TAP.2022.3222080

[11] Nesterov PK, Mizrakhy SV, Bezborodov VI, et al. Oversized waveguides as quasioptical antennas for fusion plasma diagnostics: Scale model experiment. In: Proc. of 2020 IEEE Ukrainian Microwave Week (UkrMW); 22–27 June 2020: Kharkiv, Ukraine. New York: IEEE-Institute of Electrical and Electronic Engineers; 2020. pp. 862-865. DOI: 10.1109/UkrMW49653.2020.9252689

[12] Zinenko TL, Matsushima A, Nosich AI. Surface-plasmon, grating-mode, and slab-mode resonances in the H- and E-polarized THz wave scattering by a graphene strip grating embedded into a dielectric slab. IEEE Journal of Selected Topics in Quantum Electronics. 2017;**23**(4):1-9. Art no. 4601809. DOI: 10.1109/JSTQE.2017.2684082

[13] Yashchyshyn Y, Godziszewski K. A new method for dielectric characterization in sub-THz frequency range. IEEE Transactions on Terahertz Science and Technology. 2018;**8**(1):19-26. DOI: 10.1109/TTHZ.2017.2771309

[14] Michel G, Kasparek W. Numerical analysis of complex mirror transmission lines. In: Proc. of 2008 33rd International Conference on Infrared, Millimeter and Terahertz Waves; 15–19 September 2008: Pasadena, CA, USA. New York:

IEEE; 2008. pp. 1-2. DOI: 10.1109/ICIMW.2008.4665572

[15] Liu J, Guo J, Niu X, et al. A quasi-optical transmission line for the ECR ion source. In: Proc. of 2019 44th International Conference on Infrared, Millimeter, and Terahertz Waves (IRMMW-THz); 1–6 September 2019: Paris, France. New York: IEEE; 2019. pp. 1-2. DOI: 10.1109/IRMMW-THz.2019.8874245

[16] Voitovich NN, Kazantsev YN, Tkachuk VP. Forming given directivity pattern by quasioptical line. Radiotekhnika i Elektronika. 1984;**29**(6): 1023-1028 (In Russian)

[17] Voitovich NN, Tkachuk VP, Kazantsev YN. Synthesis of quasi-optical radiating system. In: Proc. of Int. Symp. On Antennas and Propagation (ISAP-89); 1998; Tokyo. Vol. 4. Tokyo: Tokyo Univ. Publ; 1998. pp. 893-896

[18] Shatrov AD, Chuprin AD, Sivov AN. Constructing the phase converters consisting of arbitrary number of translucent surfaces. IEEE Transactions on Antennas and Propagation. 1995; **43**(1):109-113

[19] Andriychuk M, Tkachuk V. Electrodynamical model of linear array consisting of inclined semitransparent elements. In: 2021 IEEE 3rd Ukraine Conference on Electrical and Computer Engineering (UKRCON); 26–28 August 2021; Kyiv. New York: IEEE; 2021. pp. 31-35. DOI: 10.1109/UKRCON53503.2021.9575781

[20] Voitovivh NN, Andriychuk MI. Transformation of field in regular waveguide via phase correctors. In: Proc. of XIIth International Seminar/Workshop Direct and Inverse Problems of Electromagnetic and Acoustic Wave Theory (DIPED-2007); 17–20 September 2007: Lviv, Ukraine. New York: IEEE; 2007. pp. 63-66

[21] Andriychuk MI. Antenna Synthesis through the Characteristics of Desired Amplitude. Newcastle, UK: Cambridge Scholars Publishing; 2019. p. xvi+150

[22] Bulatsyk OO, Katsenelenbaum BZ, Topolyuk YP, Voitovich NN. Phase Optimization Problems. Weinheim: WILEY-VCH; 2010. p. 309

[23] Andriychuk MI. Investigation of solution of the nonlinear synthesis problem for the waveguide array. In: Proc. of Vth International Seminar/Workshop Direct and Inverse Problems of Electromagnetic and Acoustic Wave Theory (DIPED-2000); 3–6 October 2000; Lviv, Ukraine. New York: IEEE-Institute of Electrical and Electronic Engineers; 2000. pp. 47-51

[24] Andriychuk MI, Voitovich NN, Savenko PA, Tkachuk VP. Synthesis of Antennas According to Amplitude Radiation Pattern. Numerical Methods and Algorithms. Kyiv: Naukova Dumka Publ; 1993. p. 256

[25] Tkachuk VP. Frequency-phase scanning of quasioptical radiating system. Radiotekhnika and Electronika. 1986;**31**(5):877-882 (In Russian)